T0328755

A PERSON MY COLOUR

A PERSON MY COLOUR

Love, adoption and parenting while white

Martina Dahlmanns

Published in 2018 by Modjaji Books
Cape Town, South Africa
www.modjajibooks.co.za
© Martina Dahlmanns
Martina Dahlmanns has asserted her right to be
identified as the author of this work.

Edited by Emily Buchanan
Cover text and artwork by Megan Ross
Book layout by Andy Thesen
Set in Stone

Printed and bound by Digital Action
ISBN print: 978-1-928215-63-9
ISBN ebook: 978-1-928215-64-6

For L, K and N.
You are my moon, my sun and all
the stars in the universe.

With special thanks to Tumi Jonas-Mpofu
for her contributions to Part II.

Introduction

Even though we understand that the personal is political and the political personal, this is an intimate sharing of our story and not meant as a solution to current political issues. By including Tumi's story, the author appropriated a black narrative. By lending her name to the story, Tumi potentially served a white agenda.

If and when our story triggers difficult emotions, adverse opinions or outright rejection, we hope to start conversations that may contribute to our mutual learning. This would be the best outcome for us.

As much as we didn't want to hide behind the intimacy of our personal friendship, we consciously stepped away from the agenda of political correctness and allowed our feelings and instincts (and many hard conversations while walking along Sea Point Promenade) to guide us.

Whenever we got caught up in a politically correct narrative, we reminded each other of the main focus of this story, the children we both love.

We open this book with our dedications to those three beautiful humans –

Tumi writes:

When I first got to know you through your mum, who kept on inviting me to the house, I often wondered about the role I was supposed to play as a black person in your life. What was it that your mum and dad, as white parents, couldn't give you that they were hoping I would bring into your life? Was I supposed to expose you to black townships, tell you about racism, inequality, ongoing oppression? Was I supposed to role model "black success"?

Before I met you my world was pretty much reduced to shades of black and white, categorised for me by a not so long ago Apartheid government and kept in place by the reality of white privilege and continued black oppression. I did not have anything or anybody in my life to counter this reality. When I found myself in the middle of your family, my world suddenly became more complicated, not in a burdensome but in an enriching way. You added nuances and new colours to my pencil box.

I decided it would be best to go with the flow and be honest and authentic with you – and of course you always had your own ideas and questions, which sometimes threw me in a way I had not expected. Though I have no doubt that my experiences and perspectives as a black person have been and continue to be valuable for you, I realise that it is in fact you who bring something new into my life.

I can't imagine a future without knowing and loving you.

Martina writes:

A life where I might not have been your mother was never a possibility. I know today that we as a family are part of a plan born in a place and from the wisdom that our souls know as home.

I adopted you and that makes me your mother, forever, as are the women before me who gave birth to you. We are and will always be your team of mothers, none of us less real than the other. Sometimes love is a team effort by two or more mothers, or two or more parents, and there can never be too much of it. Sometimes one mother or one parent means all the love in the world. But no two mother's loves are the same and no parent loves one child in exactly the same way as they love their other child or their other children.

Mother-love is no hidden superpower, laying dormant in a woman's uterus, waiting to be activated by the process of giving birth. This is just one of the many myths (gender and sexuality some of the others) our society reinforces with moral judgements, guilt and shaming in order to keep us attached to acceptable norms.

My love does not replace or surpass your other mothers' love, a love you might only ever experience as an absence like a hole in your being. Maybe you won't. Maybe your biggest hurt is something I will never understand. This is the difficult part, where I have to witness your pain without flinching and without fixing it; where I walk by your side without being able to carry you; where I have to acknowledge my limitations and rely on other people's love for you with the hope that one day you will be able to make sense of it all.

I hope in time the world will get bored with obsessing about the many ways a family can be created. Today we are still a curiosity and a target for endless speculation. If in the years to come people look at you with judgement in their eyes or challenge you with hurtful questions, I wish for you to have the strength and speed of mind to kick their asses (literally and in other ways) until one day you might find compassion for their fears in the knowledge that – unlike them – you have been and always will be loved for who you are.

Tumi and Martina

Part I

1

Mannie

Spring 1944, Cologne, Germany

He was hiding under the big table in the middle of the camp. His safe place. The noises and smells couldn't get to him there. The plastic tablecloth came almost down to the ground, allowing just enough space to watch without being seen. It reminded him of the one that used to cover the wooden table in his mama's kitchen: shiny red-and-white checks on top, and something velvety underneath that tickled your arms and the back of your neck when you were crawling under the table.

This one was different though. The velvety side was worn out and scratchy and it gave him goosebumps when it touched his skin, like brushing against the fur of a dead dog.

He once touched a dead dog. His brother had shown it to him in a dump behind their house. The dog's eyes had been open and glassy, like those big marbles Mannie carried around in a little pouch tied to his belt that made a clinking noise when he was running. A trickle of blood glistened between the dog's yellow teeth, drawing a squiggly line down the side of its long snout. It looked mean, like its face was frozen in a permanent growl. Its thin brown fur was wet. The rain had not stopped for days. Mannie could see pale patches of skin, with crusts of dirt or old scabs. He wanted to look away, but couldn't.

His brother dared him to touch the dog.

"Coward, coward," he sing-songed over and over again. "Look at the little mummy's boy, pooping his pants."

His brother was almost eleven. Forever six years older, except for the month of October, when it was his birthday and his brother, whose birthday was in November, miraculously became only five years older.

"Look at the Hosenscheisser, pants-pooper," he snorted, spit flying out of his mouth, landing on Mannie's cheek. "Look at the poo coming out of his pants."

His brother did not like him. Mannie thought he remembered a time when there was some kind of love between them, or maybe he just dreamed it. He used to admire his brother, because he was so much bigger and smarter. But things had changed. His brother had changed. These days it seemed as if his biggest pleasure was to torment his baby brother. He also constantly acted like he was speaking to an invisible audience. Mannie was too scared to tell him how ridiculous he sounded, talking when nobody was listening.

So he'd touched the dog.

With the palm of his hand, Mannie had brushed over the part where the shoulder blades were sticking out, a goosebumpy shudder tickling down his spine. Then he ran, his feet on the wet ground, like a hand slapping bare skin, marbles klick-klacking to the rhythm of his steps, his brother's screaming laughter chasing him all the way home until he reached his hiding place under the kitchen table.

Smells of baking mixed with the faint aroma of his mother's apron, clean and fresh like spring flowers after a gentle rain. Safe. He could sit here for hours, watching his mother's slippered and stockinged feet moving backwards and forwards, drawers and cupboard doors opening and closing, the clinking of dishes, the clanging of pots, the slapping of dough on the wooden work surface between the fridge and the oven.

But these days the noises and smells were all wrong. Too many people too close together. A constant hum of voices carrying panic and fear, anger and sadness. Some never stopped sobbing; others just got angrier every day. The babies were crying all the time, night and day. There was not enough milk, his mother said. Or food.

In the past, Mannie and his friends used to run behind tractors when they came from a field with a load of potatoes during harvest time. They'd fill their pockets with the ones that jumped off when the trailer hit a pothole or a bump in the road. Mama always prepared a feast of baked potatoes with butter and salt during harvest time.

There were lots of trucks in the streets these days. They had red crosses on the sides, and big men with clean faces and shiny smiles in the back, throwing sweets at the children who ran screaming and begging after them.

Mannie hardly ever got any of the good stuff. His brother and his friends were always faster. And if he did manage to get his hands on a sweet, it got snatched from him before he could even open the blue-and-white wrapping revealing the chewy, exotic deliciousness inside.

In the camp, his brother had finally found his audience. The other kids all looked up to him. He was one of the oldest. There was no boy left over the age of 12. They'd all gone off to help Adolf Hitler win the war. They left in uniforms that looked too big on them, heads held high under heavy helmets, mothers waving handkerchiefs, eyes red from weeping. His brother turned 12 a few months ago (six years older again and no presents this year), but his Mama had somehow managed to keep him with them. Even angrier than usual, he'd started his own war, Mannie his sole enemy and all the younger children his soldiers.

Mannie could not have said how many days, weeks,

or months had passed since their house was bombed. He spent his days close to his mama. Sometimes he hid under the big trestle table in the middle of the camp, where the main meal of the day, usually a watery soup with a few limp vegetables floating around, was distributed out of a large iron pot. When everybody else had come for their soup and the women were getting ready to take what was left to the sick and elderly, he normally came out to help them. Only then did he eat his own portion with the last of the potato and carrot peels and a piece of stale bread.

Mannie couldn't remember the last time he had a slice of his mother's freshly baked bread, dripping with butter and a big chunk of salami on top.

He could feel the beginning of pins and needles creeping up his legs and bit by bit stretched them out in front of him. He couldn't risk his feet sticking out. More and more legs were slowly pushing past him. Most of the children were barefoot, feet grey from weeks without water or soap. Some had shoes on with bits of newspaper sticking out the sides, where their feet were too small, leftovers from their fathers who had "gone to war" and did not need shoes anymore.

Mannie had asked his mother where the war was, and why his father had to go there. But his mother just shook her head and said that he was too young to understand. He had asked his brother. His brother laughed at him as usual and said, "The war is in Russia, dummy, and that is further than the moon, and nobody comes home from Russia, 'cause the Russians are all monsters and we could not kill them all so we lost the war and father is not coming home, ever, cause they killed him." And he pointed his index finger at Mannie's head, thumb sticking up, "BOOM".

The procession of legs slowly shuffled along. Lots of what his mama used to call "sensible shoes": some had lost their laces; some had holes at the toes and in the soles; some, the lucky ones, had thick mismatched socks pulled over their calves. Most legs were bare, though, with red blisters and scabs, rimmed with dirt, not unlike the skin of the dead dog.

It was his mama's turn to serve soup that day. Mannie liked it when she was serving soup. Those were the days when he could sit close to her, his back almost but not quite touching her legs, a warm feeling inside of him. He forgot for just a little while where he was and how scared he was. As usual, Mama wore her slippers, the ones she ran out of the house with when the sirens were screaming. The pink fur had turned into a muddy brown, with bare patches where it has rubbed off altogether.

The dead dog again.

One of her brown knitted knee-socks had lost its elastic band and hung loose around her ankle; the other one was pulled up to her knee, where it met the hem of a brown skirt Mannie didn't recognise. It had probably come from one of the big plastic bags with clothes the men in the army trucks had dumped outside their camp the other day.

He heard the scraping sound of two wooden crutches approaching and waited for the familiar sight of an empty leg of a pair of faded grey pants, neatly folded up with two pegs swinging back and forth in front of him. If he wanted to, he could reach out and touch it with his toes, make it swing a little faster; it wasn't as if the owner would notice or even care. The corresponding leg was short and sturdy, a big army boot sticking out from under the grey fabric, frayed and blackened at the end from being dragged around in the mud for weeks.

Mannie suddenly remembered the grey pony he once saw in the circus. It could count to ten by stamping one of his sturdy front-legs, making a hollow sound and wood-shavings fly up from the floor.

The rest of the men arrived to get their soup. There were only a few of them, many of them old, sick or injured.

Some had gone to war and returned with arms or legs or eyes missing. They never spoke and they never went back to the war.

Mannie sometimes wondered if his father might come back minus a limb or an eye. He could barely remember his father. All he remembered was his deep voice and how the kitchen seemed to shrink and become darker when he appeared in the doorway. His father had gone to the war shortly after Mannie's second birthday. He had given him a grey beret with a green button on top for a birthday present. Mannie only remembered that day because he had looked so many times at the brown and beige photograph: he and his brother standing side by side in matching outfits; his brother glaring at the camera, one fist clenched by his side, the other hand gripping Mannie's chubby fingers; Mannie with his new beret on his head, smiling like a good boy, his plump legs sticking out from knee length shorts, one hand casually in his pocket, the other trustingly reaching for his brother. Mama had written on the back of the photograph: *our little sunshine on his second birthday*. His brother was not mentioned. Shortly after the photograph had been taken, his father had gone to war.

Mannie did not wish for his father to come home. He wished instead for his brother to be finally old enough to go to war, and for him and his mother to go back to their safe kitchen, where he could forever sit under the table with her fluffy pink slippers only an arm's length away. But he knew that his house had been bombed to the ground and people were whispering, "We have lost the war". His brother would never leave now.

He heard his mama talking to one of the women who had come to add more hot soup to the pot. The sick and old people, unable to walk, were still waiting in the barracks to be fed. His mama told the woman to go lie down, she'd bring her some soup later. The woman had been lying down

8

a lot, and on the rare occasions she got up, she walked slowly, folded into herself, like she had a permanent belly ache. She had lost her husband and two sons in the war.

Mannie wondered how people got lost in the war. His brother said it was just a nicer word for killed. There was often talk amongst the women about so-and-so who had "fallen in the war". If you'd "fallen" in the war, you became a war hero. Mannie did not care about becoming a hero, but he used to fall when he was smaller and he wondered sometimes how falling in the war could make someone a hero.

The woman who should lie down whispered something back to his mama. Mama told her she must look after herself and get some rest; she said she must stay strong for her boy.

The woman had one son left. He was about Mannie's age, maybe a little older. But he was small and bony, so people always thought he was much younger. Fast like a weasel and mean like a cornered rat, he was one of Mannie's brother's most loyal followers. He had made an art out of sucking snot through his nose into his mouth and catapulting it in a glob of slime at anything that moved, usually a smaller child or a stray dog.

As if conjured up by Mannie's thoughts, the Weasel was suddenly there with him under the table. He grinned his gappy grin, clearly enjoying Mannie's fear. He got ready to shout out to the world that he had found the "hosenscheisser" under the table once again, trying to hide behind his mama's skirts.

Without thinking, Mannie shoved him hard in the chest with both his fists. The other boy fell backwards, hitting his head with a cracking thump on one of the table legs, yelping like a kicked dog. With the momentum of that push, Mannie jumped up, desperate to escape to the safety of the sleeping barracks, where he'd be able to hide under one of the trestle beds before the rest of the pack came for him.

He almost made it.

His shoulder caught the table top.

The whole table jolted upwards, landing with a cacophony of splintering wood, metal spoons and bowls. Something heavy and solid hit the ground, followed by a splash and a scream that seemed to go on forever.

Mannie found himself in a muddy puddle, rolled up into a ball, pain racing up and down his back, his face pressed into his arms, hands covering his ears. Through the sleeves of his jacket, he glimpsed the woman who needed to lie down, doing just that on the ground, maybe two steps away from him. Her upper body was hidden by the upside-down soup pot, the rest of her covered in shreds of vegetables.

People came running. Within seconds they formed a wall of bodies around the never-ending scream.

Somebody called for a doctor. It was a hopeless call, a mere echo from a life where people had houses and food and shoes and dreams. Everybody knew there was no doctor, no medicine to help the woman on the ground.

Three days later the woman died. People called it a terrible accident, but everybody knew it was Mannie who had killed her. The next day a big truck with a red cross collected the Weasel. Mannie pictured him in the middle of a gigantic heap of blue-and-white striped sweets, forever feasting and spitting.

The day the woman who needed to lie down died, the little boy Mannie disappeared forever under that table, and it was the murderer Herman who jumped out and lived on to become my father.

2

The Good Girl

This is me, today, talking to the future you. Everything I say or think or dream or taste or smell or feel these days is shaped and coloured on the canvas of your being. Today, as you look at me with an open-mouthed awe only fairy-tale beings can evoke or the unfiltered hatred reserved for someone standing between you and your desire, I still rule your universe.

Often, when something you say or do, a laugh we share or a whispered conversation under your duvets at night, makes time stand still for a moment that I know will be imprinted in my memory, I wonder: will you be able to look back at this moment as part of your childhood memories, or will it simply slip away from you?

Or, instead, will you hold a miracle in your heart that I didn't even notice?

I might never know how you will remember me: which parts of our lives together will shape your childhood; what will be your happy, your scary, and your saddest moments. What I do know is that I am not the mother you will remember.

What defines me today is having you in my life: to the outside world, I am the white adoptive mother of three black children, who "looks good for her age", and who after all these years still can't shake her German accent. Because we are so obvious in our differences, I am sometimes dismissively likened to celebrities, whose names you will not even know, at other times applauded by total strangers, because I am "doing such a good thing".

I dress inappropriately for a mother my age, not because I want to prove something, but because I lack the dignified style that other women just seem to acquire along with age and status. I often look like a teenager on a budget trying out images.

On the inside, I haven't quite caught up. Middle-aged interracial motherhood might be the breakthrough role in the movie of my life, but I arrive unprepared for most of the scenes. In fact, I seemed to forget my acting skills the moment you arrived in my life.

I also have never been happier or cared less about how and what the world expects me to be, because on the inside I am simply your mother: mainly and foremost and proudly and happily and never enough so. You are the theme song to my present, already setting the mood for tomorrow, reshaping my past.

Trying to describe the "me" before you is like thinking about a relative I used to live with but hardly knew. I remember her well enough, the child, the teenager, the woman I used to be, or rather the many different roles I played. For as long as I can remember, the "real me" – the unhappy child, the angry teenager, the lonely adult – was safely locked away under many layers of appropriate responses, carefully selected to fit the requirements of whichever reality I found myself in. The face I showed to the world from early on was a paper mask covering an abomination that needed to be hidden at all costs. Something was simmering underneath the surface of my being that I felt was uncontainable, dangerous, even monstrous.

I remember most of what I did, the milestones as well as snippets of memory, like props on an unlit stage randomly appearing in the beam of the flashlight of a child playing in the dark. A feeling accompanies some of the images, like a melody played far away, evoking a sad-sweet longing for I-don't-know-what, something just out of my grasp, the memory of a memory of a feeling.

I remember the scratchy feel of my grandmother's apron against my bare legs, the sound of her voice, always on the edge of a giggle or a scream.

I was sitting on her lap, playing with little balls of white bread from the soft insides of her breakfast roll, which she was rolling and moulding with astonishing speed between her palms. Her hands were rough and red on the outside and soft and squishy on the inside. Apart from producing tiny bread balls, they could make funny squeaking noises when she pressed them together, which she often did to distract me when I was sad.

"That's for the birdies later," she would say, rolling some more bread droppings onto the table. But I knew she was just saying that so I wouldn't catch her wasting food. I had seen her throw them all in the bin.

I remember my grandfather sitting in his armchair in the dimly lit lounge, where my grandmother served him his lunch. I watched him lick his plate until it was as clean as if it had just come out of the cupboard. My grandfather had been in the war in Russia and that somehow gave him permission to lick his plate and shout.

I was not yet three years old, a blonde, blue-eyed little German prototype, proud of being called the good girl, the modest child, the clever one. It was the 1960s. My father only visited us on weekends, and my mother worked in a factory, stuffing pigs' intestines into sausages.

Until my brother arrived, and with him our new own apartment, we were living in one of two upstairs bedrooms in my grandparent's small brick house. The other room was occupied by my uncle, my aunt, and my cousin. My cousin was two years older and mostly ignored me, since she was not allowed to pile sand into my pram when I was parked under a tree for my lunchtime nap. My grandmother never called her "my good girl".

My cousin was my hero and my first love. I wished I had her for a sister instead of a baby brother. I wished he would disappear.

But I kissed his bald baby head, stroked his wrinkly little face, and smiled modestly when the adults said to each other, "Just you look at little Tinchen, how she adores her little brother."

I knew my part. I was the good girl. My mother's life depended on it.

*

3

Lena

Autumn 1944, Prussia

The little girl skipped along the dirt path leading from the farm gate straight into the shade of the nearby forest. Two older boys were walking not too far behind her, carrying a basket each. Lena loved "going for mushrooms", especially when it was just her and her favourite twin cousins. They made her laugh, chasing her through the trees and playing games, and always leaving the best finds for her.

Lena had learned from her mama how to pick the good mushrooms from the bad ones as soon as she could talk. Mama showed her the underside of each cap, letting her touch the brown-yellow sponge or riffle the papery lamellae with the tip of her finger.

"If it's a sponge, you can pick it; if it's a lamella, you must leave it."

A lamella looked a bit like the one side of the accordion her mama kept in a suitcase in the big cupboard; it could be stretched out as long as Mama's arm, making a funny sighing sound, as if trying to gobble up all the notes from Mama's sheet of music in one big breath. Sometimes, when she was "in the mood", Mama took the accordion out of its case, dusted it off with a silky white kerchief, and strapped it to her chest. She could create melodies on the accordion that made Lena dreamy and sometimes a little sad, as if she were missing someone or something she didn't even know. But when it was one of the children's birthdays, Mama always played "Happy Birthday" and other fun songs that made your feet tap and the skin at the back of your neck tingle, and everybody – her sisters, aunts, cousins, Oma, little Uncle Gunther, and even her Papa – hopped and skipped around the big kitchen table, until they fell over laughing onto chairs and each other's laps.

But on Lena's last birthday, there had been no dancing, and only the shortest "Happy Birthday" song, that didn't even sound like a birthday song. Papa's, Oma's and little Uncle Gunther's voices were missing. There was a cake with six candles, and Lena got a new summer-dress. It was yellow with white daisies and Mama had to cut up her good apron to make it. There was no money for presents and nobody even mentioned a party.

Papa had left the year before, after Christmas, just before baby Willy was born. Mama said he had to go to the war, so that they could be safe on their farm again and the bad men wouldn't steal everything. But whatever Papa was doing in the war hadn't worked. The bad men were still stealing.

Lena had never seen the bad men, but sometimes she could hear their gruff, muffled voices from the secret place in her room where you could climb into the roof through a small door without a lock or a handle; you had to push the right spot, where the wallpaper had a grubby mark between two swirls of the rose pattern, and the door magically opened with a soft click. Lena and her two younger sisters knew to go to their hiding place as soon as the village women ran past their house, skirts flying, screaming babies pressed to their chests, shouting, "The Russians are coming!" Mama and her aunts grabbed the babies and followed the women to the "dungeons" in the forest. But Oma and little Uncle Gunther always stayed behind, helping Lena and the other girls to hide in cupboards, crawling spaces, and behind the big box in the potato cellar. Because they could not run fast enough, the girls each had their hiding place in the farm house; they knew to be quiet like little mice and not come out until Oma told them it was safe again.

Oma always made sure Lena was tucked away in her secret space and gave her a kiss and a smile before she clicked the door shut and pushed the big chest of drawers in front of it. Oma was strong and never afraid. She said she was too old to be scared of boys playing at soldiers and laughed her devil-may-care laugh, waiting for the bad men in the kitchen, with little Uncle Gunther and the boy cousins, pretending to do normal things, like baking or cooking or homework.

Just before Lena's birthday, the bad men had taken Oma and little Uncle Gunther with them. Nobody knew what had happened, but when the women and babies came back from the "dungeons", and found Lena and the other girls still in their hiding places, Oma and little Uncle Gunther had vanished. The cousins told everybody that the bad men had taken little Uncle Gunther, and Oma had run after them in her house-shoes, rolling pin in one hand, shouting and pleading with them to give him back. Little Uncle Gunther was Oma's youngest son, Mama's little brother, who had come home from big school a while ago because of the war. Somebody found the rolling pin in the mud outside the cow shed, and Mama cried for days after. When she stopped crying, she had forgotten how to laugh and sing.

Lena sometimes imagined Oma in Russia with the bad men, teaching them to say please and thank you, and making them wash their hands before supper; that thought always made her feel a little less sad.

She had asked her mama why the girls had to hide from the bad men. Her mama had looked at her with that face she only made when Lena was in trouble: big cloud-grey eyes and narrow lips, the tip of her nose white, and two lines between her eyes, cutting her smooth forehead in two halves. Lena secretly called it Mama's old frown-face, but she would never say it out loud. Her mama was young and beautiful, everybody said so, especially her papa, who had been Mama's teacher at the village school and had known straight away that he was going to marry her one day. Mama always smiled and covered her cheeks with both hands to hide the pink blotches when Papa told that story.

When Mama made her old frown face this time, she didn't speak in her angry voice; instead she took Lena's face in both her hands and whispered,

"Those men hurt little girls, Lena. You must never let them find you. It would be the death of me if anything happened to you or your sisters."

The whisper scared Lena much more than the angry voice. She nodded her head fiercely, promising whatever she needed to. She would not be the death of her mama.

Lena asked the cousins about the bad men.

Maybe, the cousins said, there were not enough women in Russia or maybe the Russians liked to eat girls because they tasted better than old people or boys. The bad men were tall like giants, the cousins said, with red bearded faces and huge hands and feet. They shouted strange words, because they didn't speak German or Polish, and they all wore iron helmets, carried knives as big as axes, and smelled of smoke and whisky.

Her dad had a bottle of whisky in the cupboard in the "good room", where they celebrated Christmas and sometimes had visitors. Her cousins once stole the bottle and took it to their hiding place in the hay loft above the cow-shed, taking turns sniffing at it and pretending to take grown-up swigs. Lena had heard them cough and curse, and when she climbed up the ladder to investigate, she had seen their faces all red just like the other day, when they dared each other to eat spoonfuls of mustard straight out of the jar. So she knew not to fall for it when they tried to make her take a sip; instead she made a face at them and ran away. But for a moment, the sharp, acidic smell of the open bottle had made her nose sting; and that's how she knew exactly what the bad men smelled like. Sometimes after they had left she thought she could smell them in the pillows on her bed or the seat of the living room couch.

Lena didn't want to think about the bad men. Just for today she wanted to laugh and sing and be happy again, like she was before, just looking for mushrooms in the forest with her favourite twin cousins.

The mushrooms Lena liked best were the ones she was never allowed to pick; they were called toadstools and had shiny red caps with white dots, like a pretty flower or a ladybird. A toadstool was the most poisonous mushroom in the forest. Lena had a picture book with a tiny fairy living inside a toadstool house. It had a smoking chimney on the red-and-white dotted roof and two windows on the rounded belly of the stem with red-and-white checked curtains, and a door that looked like it was made of marzipan. Sometimes, when Lena spotted a toadstool, she lay down on the soft mossy forest floor and waited for the fairies to appear. She hadn't seen any yet, but she knew that fairies were wary of people and maybe one day, when she managed to lie still for long enough, a fairy would come.

As she got closer to the forest, Lena could see the leaves on the trees had already turned all shades of reds, yellows, and browns, as if somebody had decorated the whole forest for a birthday party.

Lena closed her eyes. She loved the feeling when the path snaked into the trees, dappling the sun light and dimming all the outside sounds: the bark of a dog on a neighbouring farm; people working in the fields; or a tractor rumbling somewhere in the distance. The air felt cooler on her face, as if she were walking into a veil of mist. The stillness of the forest, with its mossy smells of damp earth and wild berries, sometimes spiced up with the sharp tang of a fox marking his territory or furry creatures hiding in the shadows, reminded her of coming home to a kitchen smelling of Oma's baking after a long morning of sums and spelling at the village school.

Lena never minded school that much. But these days she missed her papa, who had taught the older children before he went away to the war; he used to keep a sweet for her in his jacket pocket, and let her sit on his knees and unwrap it during break time. Since her papa wasn't there anymore, the school mornings had become long and dreary, with one or the other farmer's wives taking turns teaching the children, eyes always trained on a window, looking out for bad news.

Lena walked on for a bit with her eyes closed, hands outstretched, until the boys caught up with her, each on one side, two loud "boos" in her ears.

"Hey, Kleine, are you sleep-walking?"

Lena ran away laughing, and like a rabbit being chased by farm dogs, she suddenly veered off the path and jumped across a narrow ditch that would soon become a little river. She carried on deeper into the forest, dodging trees and bushes, feeling the damp ground, squishy with soggy leaves under her black school shoes.

Lena knew she would never find the big clusters of mushrooms along a path, but had to follow her nose into the deep; and then the delight of seeing the first glistening brown hood of a cep or the buttery glow of a chanterelle out of the corner or her eye, only to realise she had stumbled upon a whole family of mushrooms hidden in the dappled light between fallen leaves and soft patches of moss; some coming up as high as her woolly knee-socks, others as small as her pinkie. She knew just how to be still and watch them emerge out of the shadows like an army coming out of the mist.

Lena kept on running, her breath like fire in her lungs, her heart beating like a fist against her ribs, the cousins close on her heels, their milk-and-mashed-potato breath the sheepskin to their wolf-cries, "Run, little red riding hood, run, before the big bad wolf gets you."

Lena screeched with glee as her hands brushed past scratchy bark and tickly leaves, collecting cool drops of yesterday's rain on her sweaty palms. She could feel someone reaching for her shoulder, a hand gripping her wrist, an arm snaking around her waist, and then they all fell to the floor in a heap of woolly limbs, laughing until their tummies hurt.

After a while Lena moved away from the boys and got up, leaving them on their backs, chewing on twigs, blue eyes roaming the sky above the tree tops, laughing and telling their stories from school: the girl they both fancied and the trick they played on Farmer Belau's wife, involving a baby pig and a freshly baked cake still in its tin. Their voices faded as she wandered off, focusing her gaze on the greens and browns of the forest floor, searching for the glimmer of a shiny brown or yellow cap.

Then she saw them. A whole family of toadstools.

And the brown and yellow pattern of her grandmother's house-dress scattered like buttercups on a meadow of moss and fallen leaves.

Lena stood still as the feeling of warm surprise at the familiar sight slowly turned into fingers of ice crawling from her stomach up her chest and into her throat. She stood still as if waiting for more mushrooms to appear from their hiding places between fallen leaves and mossy patches; only this time, she wished she could run and hide from the picture flickering unsteadily between the greens and browns and reds and yellows. Above the back of Oma's dress but somehow too far apart from it, Lena recognised her grandmother's grey-and-black bun in its torn hairnet, like a bird's nest that had fallen out of a tree, long grey strands feathering into the soggy leaves around it. The open mouth of a grey felt slipper gaped like the silent scream of a small animal and something white gleamed out of a brown lump at the end of a torn sleeve reaching towards the pretty mushrooms.

For a moment, the scene almost made sense to Lena: her grandmother lying still on her stomach on the forest floor in front of a family of toadstools, patiently waiting for fairies to appear.

Lena wanted to sink to the ground, cuddle up to the shell that once was her Oma, and see what she must have seen when she held out her hand to the magic beings.

As she felt her legs melt away from under her body, Lena heard a noise in her head, like the wail from a baby pig about to be slaughtered, and something pulled her back hard. With a silent thump, she landed on the forest floor, face buried in the scratchy wool of her cousin's jacket.

"Come away, Kleine, there are no mushrooms today. We must go home now."

Soon after that, Mama and the aunts packed everything up that would fit onto the old wagon, hitched up Papa's horse, and then they left Papa, Oma, and little Uncle Gunther behind forever. They travelled like that for a long time, always at night; they slept during the day, hiding away from the bad men in a forest hut or somebody's abandoned hay barn. Sometimes somebody offered them a bed and sometimes that same person told for a bottle of whisky or a piece of bread and the bad men found them. They never hurt Lena or the other children; they just told them to shut up. And Lena shut up and stood still, eyes firmly locked into the mouth of a black gun so she didn't have to look at her mama's face, while the bad men took turns hurting her on a floor or a stranger's bed.

Lena never went back to her forest. She grew up fast to become my fearless mama. As soon as I could talk, she took me to a forest and showed me how to look under a glistening yellow or brown cap to see if it was a sponge to pick or a lamella to leave. Sometimes I still see the ghost of a little girl in her faraway eyes, forever looking for fairies on a forest floor next to the decomposing body of her beloved Oma.

4

Versions of My Mother

1970s, Bonn, Germany

Your Oma, magical fairy storyteller from 1001 nights, bearer of gifts and gummy bears, lands in our lives once or twice a year from a different planet in her floating dresses made from rainbow-coloured silks, turbans to match, a shiny frog glinting on a finger, emerald raindrops for nails, and a giggle like a forest imp. Your love for her is uncomplicated and magnificent like a sunrise.

With her in the house, my spaces are suddenly filled with memories and miracles, shifting between moments of pure exasperation when she pushes all my forgotten buttons as only she can and a new-found peace with all that has or has not been. Her love for you is surprisingly solid and never in doubt.

So here is yet another version of my mother.

I remember her more elegant than flamboyant, a young Jackie Kennedy on the outside and burning with anger, or drowning in tears, on the inside.

It was the 1970s, and we lived in a two-bedroom apartment on the third floor of a four-storey building for government employees on a quiet and leafy street in the old capital Bonn.

Every morning I left the house at 7:15 and walked to

the end of our cul-de-sac. I crossed an unfinished building site, still deserted at this early hour, gravel crunching under my shoes, until I got to the muddy path between number 16 and 18 overgrown with rose hip bushes brushing dew drops onto my arms. I climbed over a low brick wall onto concrete pavement. With my eyes on the cracks – sometimes they had to be avoided, on other days they had to be stepped on – I walked briskly between a high grey wall to my right and bumper-to-bumper traffic to my left until I crossed to my train station in the middle of the four-lane street. I heard the screeching of steel on steel as I stepped onto the platform, just before the headlights of the red train appeared around the corner.

There were other kids from school on the train, some from my class, shouting to each other through the tunnels of interconnected carriages: homework, upcoming exams, a TV show they watched last night, and always a group ganging up and making fun of the kid that got on last.

I usually managed to melt into the background of grey business suits, open newspapers, and black combination lock briefcases somewhere in the first or last carriage.

School was a long and dreary business, with break times the twenty minutes I dreaded most. I usually attached myself to another forlorn soul with whom I had nothing in common but the wish not to be noticed and ridiculed by the "in" clique.

I still dream of trailing and trailing around that path in the schoolyard, pretending to be in deep conversation, all senses on high alert for the attack that could diminish me to a heap of rags on grey tarmac. Luckily, I was not a very interesting target and managed to stay in the shadows for most of my school career. The one time I didn't is another story I might tell you one day.

After school, I hung back as long as I could without being too obvious, pretending to look for something in my bag or tying my shoelaces while groups of kids passed me to catch the early train. I usually got onto the 13:30 train and traveled the four stations back to my stop, dreaming about a time when I would be an adult with a job, sitting in an office of my own in a grey or black suit, combination lock briefcase on my desk containing a sandwich, an apple and a newspaper.

I gauged her moods by her face as soon as she opened the door to our apartment.

There was the pinched look: sharp features carved in stone, lips glued to a thin line, eyes barely visible, scratches of ice-blue ink above her pointy nose, whiteness around the edges. That was the look that told me I had done something wrong. Sometimes silence was my punishment, or it could be the contents of my cupboard upended in the middle of the dining room floor for not having met the standards of parental inspection. I never knew which was worse, the pitiful extent of my private life in a heap between the dining room table and my sagging orange bed-couch; or the unbreathable air, leaden with my unknown offence, perhaps not even something I did but something I was. My heart sat like a rock in my chest.

Sometimes the door opened to her distant look, her public face with the perfect curve of a painted smile, chestnut-coloured hair dome towering on top of unnaturally animated features, the smell of Elnett all-weather spray, her eyes bright and bluer than a lake in winter sunshine. Her voice had a metallic ring to it, talking at me for the benefit of whoever was in the room with her or on the other end of a telephone line.

"Hello Liebling, how was school, your lunch is in the kitchen, don't forget to wash your hands," she would say, and my heart filled like a balloon, ready to burst with unspeakable emotions.

But mostly I was greeted by the weary look, exhausted

eyes brimming with recently shed tears and framed by dark circles, ragged lips soft and quivery, her body weak and dangly like a stuffed toy that's been in the wash too often. My heart would leap like a frightened rabbit in a cardboard box as I helped her onto the bed and made her cups of tea. On my lumpy couch I pretended to read, all the while listening to her soft moans, willing her not to die.

I loved her desperately. She had already gone and come back too many times to leave room for anything else inside of me but this all-consuming love. But no matter how long she was gone, I always got her back. For my love was ripping out shreds of life from my very core as daily offerings to keep her with us.

At the age of ten I knew motherhood to be a matter of life and death, something I would try to avoid at all costs.

5

Your Father Warned Me About You

I was twenty-two, the age my mother was when she found out she was pregnant with me.

The year before, I had left for Taiwan to take a three-month intensive Mandarin course at Fu-Jen language school in Taipei. This had been my last attempt to end two years of dawdling in the Sinology Department of Bonn University, not quite achieving the standard of language skills required in order to write my final exam as a translator.

I will never forget the moment I arrived in Taipei. As soon as I stepped off the airplane, the humid air enveloped me like a soft warm towel. With all the new smells and noises came the realisation that from here on everything would be utterly and wonderfully unfamiliar. But that is another story I will tell you one day, of my brief love affair with a new country, new people, a new life: the way people stared at me everywhere I went, pointing, laughing, trying to touch my hair and pale skin; the smell of diesel and wok-fried chicken; the constant noise of traffic and families living close together; how I re-invented myself through the eyes of strangers, who saw me as exotic, interesting, even beautiful – or rather how I temporarily stepped out of my cocoon and discovered I could be all these things. About the chances I took and wouldn't anymore. About the odd jobs that still make me laugh: from teaching English to business people, for whom I had to pretend to be American, to making up Chinese subtitles for Swedish porn which had been mistakenly advertised as a translation job for German short films.

Three months turned into a year full of turbulence, excitement, and exhilaration. Of course it couldn't last. Our short but regular telephone conversations left me increasingly worried about my mother and, as much as my Chinese skills had improved, I still had to write that exam to put the official stamp of approval on all these otherwise "wasted years".

So I came home.

As I had given up my small flat the previous year I moved back in with my mother for the time being. My father had also made a guest appearance. They were trying for the umpteenth time to work out their problems, or, rather, his problem of being in love with another woman.

My mother was depressed and suicidal and I still felt responsible for her survival, which in my view was solely dependent on her building a life without him, a view I had firmly held since the age of five openly and rebelliously, declaring a war against my father that I could neither sustain nor win. More or less from the moment I came into this world, inhabiting the fragile space between him and the illusion of his perfect wife, he had seen me as an intruder.

In the years to come, his resentment grew together with mine into a mutual hostility, which he disguised from himself as fatherly concern and disappointment at my many shortcomings. I always tried to get away from him. From when I was one-year-old and ran screaming from his hugs; to my awkward shuffles as a seven-year-old, when I had to kiss him good-night (a quick, dry peck on his cheek sneaking up from behind his armchair so he wouldn't be able to grab me); to my pushing the twin beds apart as far as possible in a stuffy hotel room in Prague (where he had "surprised me" for my birthday with a father-daughter weekend away but no budget for two rooms, chuckling with glee at the receptionist who had thought we were lovers); my feelings for him have always been a murky mix of guilt, fear and repulsion. Later still, supported by a therapist, I wrote him a letter, never meant to be sent. The letter ended up in a messy pile of papers in a corner of my cupboard in my Berlin flat. When I packed up all my belongings a few years later, about to start my life with your dad, it jumped out at me like a ghost from the past. Not ready to discard it but equally unprepared to carry it with me into my future, I sent it to him. For days afterwards my heart fluttered every time the phone or the doorbell rang. Even though I was trying to be realistic and grown up about it, I became six years old again, wishing for him to appear outside my front door with tears in his eyes, exclaiming, "I had no idea what you went through my darling, I am so sorry!" Maybe he would even hug me like a dad for the first time in my life before releasing me into my happily ever after.

When he called me, I wasn't prepared.

"I guess I can be thankful that you didn't accuse me of sexually abusing you," he said, adding, "Don't contact me again."

I never heard from him again, except for a gloomy black-and-white picture card on the occasion of my wedding, on which he wrote, "I hope you are happy with the decisions you made in your life and that you never regret how you treated the people in it. Your father."

So here we were again, the three of us back together (my brother was away in the army), an explosive combination: daily fights and shouting matches between my father and me, tears and threats and door slamming departures between my parents; long exhausting nights with my mother crying on the couch next to me while I desperately made up reasons and plans for her to carry on living.

Not surprisingly, I grabbed my first chance to escape this domestic nightmare. I fell for a prince ten years my senior, a travelling medical supplies salesman, friend of a friend, who said he loved me. I loved him back the only way I knew how to: desperately, painfully, exclusively, all the while waiting for him to leave me for someone prettier or funnier or more interesting.

His name was Peter. When he whispered in my ear one night in early spring, the window above my single mattress wide open to the sound of soft rain, his body warm and as close as can be, I heard, "I want to make a baby with you."

Maybe it was the magic of whispers in the dark, when the fading night brushed wings with a new morning, but his words made me feel raw and powerful like nature itself, and with the simple clarity of a dreamer I drew him into me like a patch of dry earth draws in the summer rain. As I melted into the illusion of a love so complete that it would restore myself back to me, a lifetime of control and caution flew right out the window.

He hadn't brought condoms.

The next couple of weeks he was away on business and our contact was limited to brief conversations from my parents' lounge to various pay phones throughout the country. I didn't tell him when I took the test or set up my first doctor's appointment. I told my mother, who was cautiously supportive. My father hissed and raged, "I will not have a baby screaming under my roof ever again."

I didn't care. I didn't even point out that it was neither his roof anymore nor his decision to make. I simply smiled. I was loved and I was happy.

I had a plan. There would be time enough for me to finish my exam before the baby was born, which would be around the 9th of November. We would live off Peter's salary until she was old enough to go to crèche. There was no doubt in my mind that she would be a girl. Later, I would find a job as a translator and he could finish his medical degree.

I told him in his flat under the roof of a turn-of-the-century building in Dusseldorf: lofty ceilings, old plumbing and no elevators. I had come by train, an hour huddled next to the heater of an empty compartment looking out the window through a steady curtain of rain at near empty station platforms and a cautiously green landscape dotted here and there with sheep or cows. A part of me wanted to stay on this train, suspended in time and space, safe and warm, watching the world go by and my belly grow.

For once the bus was waiting at the station and took me straight to his front door. I climbed up the five flights of stairs and let myself in with my key. The flat was stuffy and cold. I opened the door to his bedroom and put my bag on the floor next to his futon-bed. Through the narrow window I could see a patch of grey sky and down below in the courtyard an abandoned bicycle missing a wheel, leaning against a dead oak tree. Or maybe it was a chestnut and maybe it was not dead but merely waiting for an elusive spring sun to restore it back to life. I switched on the kettle and made the obligatory pot of vanilla tea, lit a tea candle for the ceramic pot-warmer, put two mugs on the table, and waited.

When I heard his steps coming up the stairs, I suddenly felt nervous.

He looked tired and older. But his face lit up when he saw me, his mouth was on my mouth, his arms around my shoulders, my face pressing against the scratchy wool of his coat, inhaling the comforting smell of his aftershave and rain and travel and his body urging me towards the bed.

"Wait," I had dreamed of saying, "I have a surprise for you."

"We will have a baby," I had practised on my way up.

"Is it safe?" he whispered instead. I nodded my head against his bare chest.

That was the last time for us. Come to think of it, that was also the last time I saw him. For when I finally told him, he looked at me with barely disguised shock. After a few everlasting seconds of silence, he said, "When I said I wanted a baby, I didn't mean with you."

I should have gone then. Should just have got up, dressed, grabbed my bag, and left.

But I didn't.

Instead I did what I had watched so many times growing up, an ever-expanding ice-block of fear and contempt in my chest: I tried and pleaded in a feeble attempt to resuscitate my expired hope for a happy ending. The afternoon turned into a night of tears and words like hurled rocks that did not leave any visible bruises, as I watched myself with unbelieving horror turning into a carbon-copy of my mother re-enacting the theme song to my childhood.

He escaped to work early the next morning with a final blow, "Your father warned me about you." I put the keys on his desk calendar, flipped forward to the 9th of November and made a red cross on the date. Then I left.

On the train ride back, the sun was shining. I leant my hot forehead against the cool glass of the train window and closed my eyes to the beautiful spring morning.

6

Becoming Myself

The abortion was a relief. When it was finally over, after five or six weeks of bureaucratic appointments, repetitive statements and disappointed stares from doctors and nurses, my mother's helpless silence and my father's relieved unease, my brother picked me up from the anonymous clinic, harmlessly hidden away between farm buildings, cow-sheds and apple orchards. His red VW Beetle had its top down. It was a beautiful sunny day, unusually warm for late April. The air had that fresh early summer smell of cut grass and apple blossoms.

He greeted me with his familiar look of exasperated brotherly worry. There was also a flicker of fear in his voice when he asked me how I was, as if I had an explosive device strapped to my belly that could go off at any minute. I said I was fine and I meant it. He took the tricky bends on the narrow country roads too fast and we nearly ended up in a ditch next to a field of happy cows, drunk on bellies full of fat green grass and their new-found freedom after a long winter confinement. I laughed at their impassive, somewhat snobbish expressions, his mortified apology, and the irony of it all.

We had never learned to be close.

Being around him always made me slightly uncomfortable. I could never quite shake an oppressive sense of responsibility for our strained relationship or my guilt for not loving him enough. Behind his grown-up façade, I still saw the four-year-old little boy who followed me around everywhere needing comfort, constant attention, and so much more than I could cope with; or the skinny eight-year-old who hung around my girlfriends and me, desperate for acknowledgement and playmates. I was battling my own demons, and mainly ignored him or joined in when they made fun of him.

He was also the good son for whom I had messed up everything.

"Why can't you just be quiet for a change and not destroy everything?"

I could still hear his anxious, desperate twelve-year-old voice one Christmas Eve as I got into yet another fight with my father, who was preaching his disappointment at me for not having the camera ready for family pictures. Since I had been presented with this unwanted instrument a couple of birthdays ago, it had become my responsibility to take pictures of all the momentous family occasions.

Of course, as with the cupboard that somehow never stayed tidy, I made a mess of things: the camera stopped working and I never got it repaired.

I meant to, I truly did.

But in all the months leading up to Christmas, I had managed to avoid thinking about it, knowing full well that it would all blow up in my face on Christmas Eve. When it did, when the precariously maintained family truce was shattered by my father's outburst, calling me irresponsible, negligent, and undeserving of such an expensive gift, I calmly looked at him and said, "Why don't you just use last year's pictures, it's all the fucking same anyway."

He slapped me then, as I knew he would.

I stayed outwardly distant and calm, feeling the grim satisfaction of exposing him as the abuser he was.

Between my mother's sobs and my father's rage, I heard, above all, my brother's despair and helpless fury with a sister who couldn't just for once keep quiet and play along.

He ran out of the house that cold winter night, in just a shirt and his slippers. My parents didn't even bother to worry about him; everybody was too caught up in their own inner hell. He must have come back eventually, but I don't remember how or when.

Being in the car with him on this sunny afternoon after my abortion felt like a replay of our childhood theme. As usual, I had broken the rules, messed with the somnambular peace of the established. As usual, I had gotten into trouble.

After the near accident, we didn't speak much. As soon as we got home, I lay down on my freshly made bed, nightgown laid out for me, a bunch of garden flowers in a vase on my night-table. I fell into a deep dreamless sleep.

When I woke up the next morning, it was with an overwhelming feeling of relief: the nightmare was finally over. My body was my own again, the last trace of Peter gone. There was also the relief of not finding myself on my mother's path. As I was lying on my bed, the faint hiss of medicated pain deep inside of me, I had the first glimpse of the possibility of becoming myself.

I also knew without a trace of guilt or doubt that I was not ready to be a mother.

Any thoughts of my unborn children were strangely peaceful and forgiving. It was the first time I got a sense of the timeless wisdom at the very root of my self, a voice as fleeting as a feeling from a dream, and at the same time a strong and powerful knowing: if being a mother meant burdening a child with my unlived life, and the helpless rage of an abusive stranger who called himself father, sending it away was what ultimately saved us all.

7

Not a Bad Place to Be

I met a boy and followed him to Berlin; experimented with freedom, friendships, love and drugs; realised I didn't like drugs the same time I realised I was in love; tried to pretend otherwise; got a job taking rich people around China; found out from my gynaecologist that my boyfriend cheated on me (*no sweetheart, you can't get this from a toilet seat*); left him and tried to be gay; kissed a girl but lost my nerve; got fired and took my employer to court; they paid me a lot of money to go away so I went travelling through Thailand and Indonesia; fell in love with a man from Switzerland and left him in Singapore so he would not break my heart; found out that breaking my own heart hurts just as much, with no one to blame but me; came home to Berlin and allowed the boy who cheated back into parts of my heart and my apartment; took up new studies, a new job, and a new lover with a talent for carpentry and a drug habit; broke up with the boy who cheated and let a coin decide who was going to move out the next day, heads up meant I could stay; he stormed out the same night, came back several times, either suicidal or murderous in his rage, kicking down my front door for good measure, which, lucky me, my talented lover repaired the same day. I felt safe with him, because I wasn't alone.

So when he hit me, I didn't see it coming. The first slap exploded in my ear like a gunshot. It took me a while to connect the sound to my burning face and still I did not understand. I felt like I had just woken up from an afternoon nap to a scene from a B-grade movie playing at full volume. With a mixture of fascinated disgust and detached suspense, I rubbed my eyes and tried to make sense of the action, before I realised I was in it.

I made all the right moves that first time. I kicked him out, screamed at him, slammed the door in his face and ignored his calls. A few days later he stood in the courtyard of my block of flats, underneath my bedroom window, presenting round-eyed excuses, a cake he had baked for me, a heart shaped balloon and a sunflower. I took him back without thinking, overwhelmed by his efforts, the real tears in his eyes and the newness of an abuser apologising to me. Until the next time. And the next. He didn't always hit me. Sometimes it was just a glass smashed against the wall, or a threat disguised as a joke (you'll learn to fly before you leave me) as he held me tight next to an open third-floor window.

There was that moment when I came home from work and didn't make it up the stairs, worried he might still be there from the night before. He had tried to rape me on the bathroom floor but was too high to go through with it and instead ripped the telephone cable out of the wall so I wouldn't call the police. I found myself staring at the window display of a gun-shop a few blocks down from my apartment, weighing up the benefits of a jack-knife versus a can of mace versus a gas pistol.

I wish I could tell you I left him that day with a final act of strength and retribution. But for a while I was more scared of being alone than I was of being thrown out of a window. I made too many excuses and accepted too many apologies and after all, I was not weak, nor a victim. The drama also kept me from looking too deep and thinking too hard.

I did what I do best. I came up with a plan to reinstate the illusion of being in control. I realised that the intensity of his outbursts was directly related to the drugs in his system and learned to read the signs over a telephone line. I avoided him when he was high on coke and got him to smoke weed with me instead. Without the necessary fuel his rage dimmed down to a not-so-life-threatening version of occasional sneering contempt.

It never came to a final showdown. Our passion slowly leaked away and what remained was boredom and empty silences. After yet another half-hearted fight and his remorseful performance that fell as flat as an overused cliché, our break up was as unspectacular as leaving a hotel room after a disappointing holiday. Resentful, but also relieved, we both packed our bags and left.

Soon after my life came to a stop, like running full speed into a glass wall.

I woke up one morning with dry burning eyes and a strange taste in my mouth. When I looked in the bathroom mirror, my eyes stared back at me unblinking from behind a mask of vaguely familiar features, like somebody had stuck a layer of cling-wrap over half my face while I was sleeping.

The doctor next door went pale with shock and sent me to a neurologist. They thought it was a stroke. They said I had a sixty per cent chance of recovery, which to me meant that in all likelihood my life was over. They gave me vitamins and a sheet of paper with drawings of weird facial expressions, sets of exercises for me to do each day.

I had to close my left eye with my fingers at night, cover the left side of my face in the shower so the spray would not hurt my eye-ball, and drink coffee through a straw. Food tasted like cardboard soaked in water and most of it fell out of my mouth as I was chewing. I left my apartment once a day to walk to the neurologist's practice, where I lay staring at the ceiling for three hours hooked onto a vitamin B drip, crying tears I could not feel. The nurses tried to communicate with me while giving me helpless pats and looks of pity as I rolled words around my tongue which lay beached in my mouth like a dying whale.

The rest of my days I spent in front of the TV, monitoring my face every few minutes in a small make-up mirror. I found a strip of four passport pictures taken in one of those instant photo booths and cried over all the possibilities in my eyes and my lost smile.

I stopped answering my phone and people stopped calling, except for Inge, who did not leave the entrance of my building until somebody buzzed him in and then hammered on my door until I opened it.

I had known Inge since he came to Berlin a few years back. He had grown up not far from my own neighbourhood in suburban Bonn and had moved to Berlin to avoid conscription (Berlin citizens were exempt from army duty). He was the dorky childhood friend of somebody from my volatile circle of party-hipsters, who had left him on my doorstep (*you have so much in common*) like an unwanted puppy. When I first met him, he had no friends and a boring job, and wore his innocent small-town charm like a favourite hand-knitted jersey. Despite my fashionably groomed aloofness, he had stuck around like a friendly stalker, and after a year or two, I had come to rely on him as a party companion and shoulder-on-call whenever I was in the midst of yet another drama.

In time, he learned how to fine-tune his pretty looks to acceptable standards with the right amount of hair gel, facial hair, and labels. He drove a vintage Merc which took us in style to parties, nightclubs, and weekend outings. He was thin and wiry with the nervous energy of a hungry greyhound, constantly requiring food but never gaining weight. Before an outing, I always kept a Mars Bar and a Rolo in my handbag to keep his temper on an even keel. Inge also had a love for Greek food, Monty Python movies, MTV, and girls who did not love him back. I told him

I only went for the bad guys, as if it was a joke, and that he was too good for me. He accepted my rejection as if he had expected nothing else and we remained as we were.

When Inge hammered on my door that day, I knew it could only be him (or the police); nobody else would have visited without a screening-call first.

I opened the door without looking at him and went straight back to bed. He tried not to flinch when he saw my face, made me get dressed, and dragged me through cold deserted streets to our favourite Greek restaurant. I sat next to him so he would not look at me and he ordered all our favourite dishes: dolmades, spanakopita, moussaka, tzatziki with soft white bread, and white wine with a straw.

I noticed the old couple sitting next to each other at a table across from us just as a tasteless bite of soggy bread was dropping out of my mouth. She was giggling at something (me – I suspected), a tinkling sound that reminded me of the little bell my father used to ring at Christmas. Her arms were hanging by her sides like branches broken off a tree, half of her mouth pointing down in a permanent scowl while the other half was plucked by invisible strings into a twitchy dance. He was patiently feeding her small forkfuls of food, his face shining with tenderness.

I stared at them in shock and disbelief. All I could see was a harrowing vision of myself 30 or 40 years from now, and I turned to Inge, ready to get up and storm out, back to my apartment, never to leave my bed again.

He looked at me, eyes wide with panic, making choking noises. I was about to hit him between the shoulder blades or call for help when a spray of breadcrumbs flew in my face and I realised he was laughing so hard that he had tears in his eyes and veins popping on his forehead. He laughed his great big Inge-laugh, reminiscent of road-trips singing along to Guns N' Roses in German (which is only funny for Germans) or discovering a Rolo-sized chocolate stain on the backside of his white pants after leaving a trendy Berlin art gallery.

Before I had time to get mad, I felt a giggle like a hiccup bubbling up my throat and tumbling out of my mouth in an exhilarating outburst of unhinged freedom, like hurtling down a black ski-slope in a cardboard box. The old couple looked at us, mild surprise in their eyes, and then he smiled as if someone had just told his favourite joke and placed another forkful of food in her lopsided mouth.

Later, we staggered out of the restaurant, holding onto each other as we made our way back to my apartment over icy pavements, wintery smells of coal ovens and exhaust fumes in the air, laughter drifting into the darkness in puffs of white cloud.

That night I woke up and felt my eyelid twitch for the first time in months.

It turned out my stroke was a nasty virus and in time I would recover.

Slowly and imperceptibly at first, as winter turned into spring, my face unfroze and the mask melted away. My life went back to its previous rhythm of work and study interspersed with a borderline-pathological love life, but everything felt different, like a familiar food that no longer tastes the same.

There was a sentence stuck in my head, like an advertising jingle playing over and over again: *If you don't listen now, the next time you won't get away so lightly.*

Listen to what, I had no idea. I only knew the mask had not been me and what was underneath, I did not recognise. Somehow I had to find a way back to myself.

As a peace offering to the universe, I went to see a therapist with a flowery name. She was my mother's age with kind eyes, doughy features, floating dresses and sunny rooms on the sixth floor of an Art Deco building with no elevators and a chair on every second landing. Climbing up to her apartment once a week was like ascending into a parallel universe in which I became the child that I had never been: clingy, weepy, desperate, hopeless and needy.

Rosa gave me tissues, awkward (for me) hugs, and unconditional love every Wednesday from four to five, sometimes an additional hour on a Friday. At times the chair opposite hers was my raft, tossed by waves of inexplicable sorrow or boundless rage, with no words and no memories, anchored only by her unflinching gaze. At other times, I simply sat mute and isolated on my floating island, framed by dark skies and no horizon, with my story ripped from me and nowhere to go.

"Not a bad place to be," Rosa said, and I felt peaceful and weak like a child all cried out. "Anything is possible from here on."

8

Then I Met Your Dad

1995, Cape Town

So I grew up.

I got my degree in communications, broke up with my lover, most friends, my boss and my father, and rewarded myself for all of the above with a two-week trip to South Africa where my brother had studied medicine. I had refused to visit until Nelson Mandela was freed. The day had come and gone and like South Africa I felt newly liberated and somewhat reborn (in a strictly non-religious way) so I finally made that visit.

We travelled together for two weeks, Matt and I, made a new, grown-up peace with each other, and then I watched my plane leave without me from a bright orange towel on Camps Bay beach. I found a job (another story to tell you one day) and gave myself a year in which to experiment with life.

Then I met your dad.

He was the kind of man I might warn you about. Tall and crookedly handsome, with no identifiable profession, he roamed the streets in his vintage two-seater BMW, attracting jealous stares and dubious desires. The day I met him in my new job as an office-admin-accountant-assistant in an edgy designer business, run by an equally edgy and beautiful

German my age, I could not have been worse prepared. Two men-in-black, who had arrived as customers but then turned out to be Home Affairs officials, had threatened me with imminent deportation unless I could produce a valid work permit or business visa within 24 hours, neither of which was likely to happen.

My boss Linda was trying to calm me down when he came up behind her with a bear hug that almost enveloped us both and a wink and a smile saying he had intended just that. I inhaled the smell of him (polished leather with traces of smoke from a camp fire) and drank in his eyes, the colour of a forest lake glinting with mischief under an eternally benevolent sun, as if a magic spell had heightened all my senses. Looking back, I mostly contribute this effect to the adrenalin rush brought on by my near-deportation experience, but maybe, just maybe, the heavens really shifted and allowed me a glimpse into what my life could feel like with him in it ...

Steeped in confidence, dismissively conscious of his impact on the world in general and my deeply shaken self in particular, he rested his chin on Linda's golden head and said to me, "It looks like you're in trouble, anything I can do to help?"

"Sure, you can marry me."

The joke fell flat as soon as it came out of my mouth, like a baby bird on its first flight attempt. I felt my face burn with a rising blush. He gazed at me, smiling as if contemplating my proposal for two, three, four held breaths during which I failed to come up with anything at all to say.

"Yeah, well, I am not sure I want to go down that road anytime soon," and with a giggle he released Linda so she could turn around and peck him on the cheek.

"Hi darling, I don't think you have met? This is Martina, she just started working here," and to me, "This is Alan, my export partner."

"Nice to meet you," I breathed, "I'll let you two talk." I swiftly turned towards my office where I put my head on the desk and hoped to disappear in a puff of smoke.

Instead, my visa problems got sorted out by a competent lawyer, courtesy of my connected boss, and your dad kept visiting, which I attributed solely to Linda's beauty and their business connection. Well-trained in Berlin social etiquette, I made a good show, or so I thought, of ignoring him after a perfunctory greeting. I pretended to be on the phone or otherwise busy with something on my computer screen.

After a few weeks of a steadily decreasing interest in food, day-dreams featuring your dad and a swimmy feeling in my head whenever he entered my cubicle, I had to admit to myself that I was once again falling for the wrong guy. With all the wisdom from Rosa still fresh in my mind, I resisted a good while longer, which only seemed to increase his visits and my kamikaze longing. What I thought was my secret alone, I soon found out had been glaringly obvious to everyone else. Linda begged me to have him already and get it over with. My lovelorn existence was bad for business and at least I could start to recover after being ditched.

When he finally called me one day and asked to "pick my brain" with regards to a new business venture, I, unacquainted with English idioms, thought this to be a clever pick-up line, and got dressed for a date. He brought along papers and catalogues and figures and timelines and, when I realised my mistake, we were already halfway into starting a furniture business with me still as hopelessly smitten as before.

Today he tells me he only planned the business so he could spend time with me (and I am starting to believe him), but what I remember most are my Sleeping Beauty swoons and his dashing smile and good eye for an opportunity.

Maybe I am not doing justice to our love story, and one day your dad will tell you his version.

9

You Should Marry Him

April, 2004

I like to imagine this day as the day Lele was conceived. We were walking along our favourite beach, your dad and I, holding hands and chatting like we did most Monday mornings while the rest of the world was at work (after all, we started this business so we could be together and never work on Mondays).

We had been living together for close to eight years, in a brown ginger-bread house from the '50s or '60s on the slopes of Signal Hill with lots of corners, mouldy carpets, and a steep roof topped by candy-green tiles like cracked icing. We bought the house before property prices boomed and white South Africans slowly realised they were not going to be chased away by their formerly oppressed house-keepers and gardeners. It was not our good instinct for an investment opportunity that made us put down an offer on our rented home; we simply loved it too much to move out when the owner mentioned he was going to sell soon. We had also just got married, our business was booming, and buying a home seemed the right grown-up move to make.

The marriage proposal had come about in the kitchen of my old flat in Berlin in the wake of one of our epic fights.

When I decided to stay in Cape Town, I had sublet my flat to a friend on the condition that I could stay there on occasional visits. Alan and I stayed in Berlin for a stopover on our way to Denmark for the wedding of my new friend Bella, who was also your dad's ex-girlfriend. Just in case you think our fight had anything to do with this, it didn't.

Our fights, as far as I remember, had no theme or reason to them; they erupted like wildfire after a drought on Siberian grasslands. There was no warning, no sudden drops in mood or spikes in temperature, and no animals ran for the hills. Our fights were seasonal and when the time had come, any careless spark could start a raging fire, only to be smothered some sleepless nights later by a tear-soaked reunion. As the years went by, we learned to take some precautions, including week-long sessions with a doe-eyed therapist couple in their little house which crouched like an enchanted mushroom in a forest in Germany, candles flickering in narrow passages and smelling of old churches, wet moss and home cooking.

The first question they asked us, perching on their matching chairs like a pair of doves, eyes bright and alert – *Do you want to stay together?* We answered without thinking – *Yes*. After that, things became more complicated.

They taught us to hit pillows and listen to each other in order to lengthen and strengthen the seasons between disasters. I learned things about your dad that he hadn't had words for, and he followed me to my cracked and dusty shell where he curled up next to me. I felt comforted and held like the earth had opened up and moulded itself around us.

Eventually we got better, individually and as a couple. Still, it took us many years to realise the earth did not have to shake for us in order to prove we could hold onto each other. For as long as they lasted, our fights never lost their all-consuming intensity, and each time I made frantic escape plans in my head, accusing your dad of the same. Each time he looked at me, eyes round with disbelief and said, "Leaving you is not an option. I am never leaving you. How can you even think that?"

For the next few days after that, we were Adam and Eve and Romeo and Juliet: fragile but strong, bruised but new, washed out but aglow with a secret too precious to expose in a world of Hollywood endings and reality TV romances.

Back in the kitchen of my old flat in Berlin, leaning against one of my ice-cream-coloured retro chairs, a weak April sun hovering outside the windows too high up to ever be opened or properly cleaned, I was convinced there was something unfixably wrong with our relationship or with me. Your dad had spent the morning on top of the No. 1 bus, circumnavigating the city centre a number of times, sulking from Bahnhof Zoo via Ku'damm to Alexanderplatz and back.

I had found temporary shelter in my old refuge, the chair opposite Rosa, with an emergency appointment.

"I can't do this," I sniffed as soon as I entered the room and sat down in my chair, reaching for the box of tissues I knew was on the floor next to it.

"I tried, I really did, but it is just too much for me. Too much pain, too much fighting, too much … feelings; I don't know what's right anymore, everything is just … wrong." I blew into a handful of tissues and looked up to meet her eyes, steady and unruffled like a mountain pool and as familiar as gazing at myself in a mirror.

After a blink or two I looked away again, as I had always done, unable to sustain eye contact throughout our mounting silences.

Everything was as it had always been: long stretches of quiet, her eyes warm on my face, searching for the answers only I had; the old-fashioned chrome wall clock behind her ticking away slow seconds; a light breeze coming from the window she kept ajar at the first sign of spring; bird families chirping from their treetop homes below us, and much further away, the sound of traffic, a constant hum interrupted by the occasional hooting or slamming of car doors; the faint smells of Rosa's musky perfume and something vanilla and flowery coming from an oil burner on the windowsill next to a tear-shaped blue ceramic bowl holding twigs of apple blossoms like snowdrops on a glassy sea.

"I think I have to take a break from relationships altogether," I eventually said, my voice raspy as if I hadn't spoken all day. "I have been with one guy or another ever since I was sixteen. I have never really been alone ... I think I need to learn how to be alone. I need to be able to be OK by myself." I heard the whine of a tired five-year-old in my voice as I contemplated the shelf next to her, crammed with books by Alice Miller and Fritz Perls, little figurines of angels and Buddhas and a framed picture of a turbaned man with a beard: her Indian guru, she had once told me in a rare moment of self-disclosure.

Still she did not talk. When I looked at her again, I saw a tentative smile spread across her face, which I now noticed was a little more lined and a little more tired than I remembered. "I wonder ..." she finally said with that soft, pondering tone I knew really meant *I think you're wrong*. "Have you really never been alone?"

On that note, all my ghosts entered the room: the forgotten baby, unloved child, lonely sister, betrayed friend, and some I didn't even recognise. They all filed past me hand in hand, reminding me with their downturned faces and hidden eyes that I could not bury them again, their strangely triumphant parade almost daring me to try.

"Maybe you need to learn how not to be alone instead?" Rosa waved them all away with a bit of magic dust from her peacock-coloured scarf and I rubbed my eyes and stretched my limbs like I had just woken up.

"But what if I can't, what if it's too late?" I whispered, crouching in my chair and playing with my fingers, feeling like the five-year-old who still thinks that Mama has all the answers.

"Martina, can I say something to you?" she asked me and the strange note of uncertainty in her voice made me sit up and look at her again.

"I have never done this before and would not normally do this, but I have a feeling I won't see you again and you should hear this from me." She searched my face as if to gather strength for what she had to say.

"OK." I breathed in deeply and held onto the arms of my chair, trying a joke to diffuse my anxiety, "Is there any way I can say no?"

We both smiled like two old friends sharing an amusing memory and then she said to me, "You should marry him."

When I got back to the flat, the first thing I heard was the whistle of the old kettle, a big-bellied silver and black affair I inherited from the couple who had lived there for 50 years before me. When they moved out (because he could no longer climb the stairs to the third floor), I found old tins of paint and outdated gadgets stacked under the kitchen sink, all neatly wrapped up in bits of newspaper from the '60s. I spent a day unwrapping stuff and reading all the articles like entering a time tunnel, entertaining happy visions of myself and the boy-who-cheated and what we might leave behind 50 years from then. Not much, it turned out. But I kept the kettle.

As I followed the sound of the whistle into the kitchen, I found Alan buzzing about, the aroma of coffee grains and burned oil from years of cooking on the antique gas stove competing with a wave of fresh aftershave, which told me he had just had a shower. He greeted me with a cautious smile, trying to gauge my mood as he joked about spending the morning searching for the "Bundeskartoffel-Amt" (Ministry of Potatoes), mimicking people's replies in his version of a German accent, which usually never failed to make me laugh. But that day Rosa's words rang like church-bells in my head (*marry him, marry him, marry him*) and I was lost for words or smiles.

I burst into tears.

That stopped him mid-sentence.

"Are you still mad at me?"

"No," I sobbed.

"Why are you crying? Is it my German accent?"

"I don't think I can be in a relationship." I wiped my face with my woolly sleeve, and rubbed the sleeve on my jeans, avoiding his eyes. "I don't know how to. I mess everything up. I think I need to be alone." Still I didn't look at him.

"Is that what you want?" he asked, serious now.

I shook my head, contemplating the snot stain on my pants leg.

When he didn't say anything, I looked at him, my vision blurred by new tears, and blurted out, "Rosa thinks we should get married."

He took two steps and wrapped me in his arms.

"OK," he said, "let's get married."

"OK," I whispered into his armpit.

And that was that.

Six years later, we were walking on our favourite beach in Noordhoek.

I had received an email from Inge the day before, untypically philosophical and introspective, which he had written on a long train ride through colourless German landscapes, depressed under a permanent layer of cloud. His musings covered dark skies, long ago road trips, and nights we spent watching MTV before hitting the club scene at four am. He ended with: *There are so many people out there* (on the station platforms, I guessed) *who have children, but they all look like horrible parents who will only bring up more horrible people (what is the point of it all?). And you two*, he went on, addressing Alan and me, *who would be great parents, don't want children ...*

We had had conversations along those lines before, Inge and I, and he knew my position well, so he finished with his own punchline, which I repeated to your dad just as we were about to reach our turning point, a large seal-shaped rock at the end of the beach.

"So Inge says to me, maybe you are right and you really don't need children to be happy, but have you thought about the possibility that a child might need you to be happy?"

To the sound of waves echoing the rhythm of our easy chatter, and the early morning sun throwing silver sparkles all around us, Inge's words rose up from the sea in a burst of glitter, hovered over the horizon for a few blinks, and then dissolved in a spray of foam: *a child might need you to be happy.*

It really was as easy and simple and magical as that.

"Maybe he is right?" Your dad turned towards me. With the sun behind him, I couldn't quite read his face but there was a tremble of excitement in his voice.

"About what? Us being good parents?" I kept my voice light, not sure whether that sizzle in my blood was panic or joy.

"Yes," said your dad, "I think we are ready for our own family."

"OK," I said, and, "We are adopting, right?"

"Of course."

For a while we just walked, hands clasped, working a little harder as the sand grew softer under our feet and the sun shone in our eyes. Two over-enthusiastic Labradors ran circles around us and I almost wanted to glare at the owner for trespassing on our moment, but I couldn't convince myself, and that was when I realised I was happy. After a lifetime of running and fighting and wondering, it only took the thought of you for me to know happiness.

10

Paper Pregnant

It took us nine months from that walk on the beach in early April until you were placed in my arms in January, my own version of a perfect pregnancy.

The adoption agency called it paper pregnant. We called it a paper infestation. Papers were scattered on tables and shelves, spilling onto the floor and sticking out from under seat cushions. There were forms to fill in, reference letters we had collected from friends and family a "person in your community who is neither a friend nor a family member," glossy adoption agency brochures, stapled information sheets on "What to Expect When You Are Adopting" and questionnaires the size of complicated vacuum cleaner manuals (and as eye-wateringly tedious) to establish our mental, emotional and relationship health.

Sitting on the carpet in front of the coffee table, overcome with nerves at the bureaucratic seriousness of it all, your dad and I distracted each other by coming up with alternative answers to some of the more bizarre questions, which we had to answer on a scale from one ("strongly disagree/never") to five ("strongly agree/all the time"). It felt like thousands of ticks, each heavy with meaning, a secret code a nameless person in an office, who had never met us, would translate into a life changing decision on our behalf. I felt slightly guilty, like I was trying to cover something up.

"Do you sometimes think about killing yourself?" Alan read out to me.

"Yes, sometimes, when filling in questionnaires," I answered without looking up (a tick for "strongly disagree/never").

"Do you sometimes use violence to solve problems?" I picked for him.

"I only ever punch fellow drivers who stop in the middle of the road to ask for directions."

He grinned at me as we both remembered the time last year when a BMW had cut him off in rush hour traffic and instead of apologising the (white, middle-aged) driver flipped his middle finger out of the car window. Alan got out of his car at the next traffic light, calmly walked over to the BMW and bent both windscreen wipers until they stood out like feelers on a praying mantis . He told me about it later that day, still laughing. We both ticked "strongly disagree/never" on our respective forms.

"Do you sometimes feel unable to get out of bed?" He wiggled his eyebrows at me.

"Only after a night of heavy drinking."

"Do you use recreational drugs?" He pretended to tick the "sometimes" box and waited for me to punch his arm away, so I could insert the correct answer for him.

Then there were the sneaky I-statement questions meant to trip us up, a page or two further down, just in case we forgot that we lied five minutes earlier.

"I sometimes feel life is not worth living," he found for me.

"Just about right now," I added the tick.

"I think corporal punishment is appropriate when disciplining children." Your dad was on a roll.

"Strongly agree. I hit mostly other people's children though, as I don't have my own yet," I responded.

"I sometimes feel overwhelmed when thinking of my

day ahead." I beat him to that one.

"I quickly smoke a doobie when that happens." He took his pen between thumb and index finger, mock smoking a joint. We both ticked our respective boxes.

"What type of hair do you want your child to have?"

Three options: straight, curly or either.

"How do they know what type of hair a child will come out with?" I asked your dad, still oblivious to the undertones of a racist society.

"Oh they're just saying that so you don't have to come straight out with it, if you don't want a black child." Matter-of-fact.

We had not explicitly discussed the "race issue" but, living in a country where less than ten per cent of the population was white, we both assumed that our child would be brown or black. I am embarrassed to admit it, but my stance at the time was the colour-blind attitude unconscious racists all over the world employ: black, white, yellow, purple, I don't mind what colour my child has, love has no colour (insert the monkey-covering-eyes emoticon here).

After the hair question, just to spell it out for the not-so-together adopters, straight to the next point, "What complexion do you want your child to have?" The options: fair, medium, dark ... But isn't this the same question?

I felt uneasy then for the first time, as if I was selecting a child like a piece of furniture from a catalogue. Maybe it was the first time I felt like a mother, angry at a system that reduced my child to a box, an item to be categorised and rejected if no fit was established. I wanted to protect you from the boxes. As a small act of defiance, I didn't tick any. I don't know if I'd already felt the first hint of doubt back then, filling in those questionnaires and forms. Maybe it was just a brief unease, as I glimpsed out of the corner of my eye an ugly and dangerous parallel universe before quickly looking away again. There was something intangible yet pervasive in the air around me which knotted my insides and made my skin crawl, as if somebody had broken into our house, spied in my cupboards, touched my clothes and rubbed themselves against my bedsheets.

The rest of the process was uneventful. Two social workers visited us at work jokingly checking-but-not-checking if we had "a roof over our heads". They took our word for it.

There was the pre-adoption meeting with another social worker, who prepped us for all sorts of scenarios which went right over my head: bonding difficulties, stranger reactions, possible rejection from within our families, post adoption blues. Never once was race mentioned. When we got home I remembered her request to compile a profile for your birth mother. The implication was the prettier the profile, the quicker we would be chosen by someone who would give us her child. I made you a yellow box with pictures, little gifts and letters from family and friends, all welcoming you. I also added a diary and a photo album with pictures of your dad and me as children, as adults, after we met and when we got married. I left blank spaces for your picture for "when we had you". I wrote a letter to your mum. I wrote you a letter. I called you Lele.

11

Lele

The evening before we brought you home, we walked on the beach again, your dad, Wilma (our first dog) and I. There is a picture that shows me sitting in the sand, one arm around Wilma, my face next to hers. The setting sun dips us in shades of pink and gold, my short hair almost the same length and colour as her orangey brown fur. Like we belong in a coffee table book of "people who end up looking like their dogs," we both grin broadly into the sun. I look at this picture today with a longing for the innocence of this evening; the happy expectation of you as a simple and all-consuming joy, like being a child again on the evening before Christmas.

We spent the rest of the evening reminding each other that this was the last time it would be just us: our last evening of being a couple on the couch watching a movie, our last night sleeping without our child, our last morning coffee in bed, our last breakfast alone. A happy series of lasts that made me feel giddy and a little boisterous, like I'd had a strawberry daiquiri before supper.

Then it was the next day. When we left the house, I felt happy and excited. A little nervous too, but it was the kind of nervous that tickles your insides in the way a ride on a roller coaster does. As I was coming down the steps from our front door, empty baby carrier over my shoulder, your dad filmed from below, giving a live commentary, "Here she leaves the house, bag still empty. When we next make our way back up these stairs, it will have our baby in it."

That sentence, delivered with a smile and a wink, threw me off balance. The reality of the empty baby bag suddenly became overwhelming and daunting. I quickly dropped it on the back seat and buckled up, willing myself to breathe, to not think about passing out in the waiting room of the adoption agency or doing something equally embarrassing that would prove I was not fit to be your mother after all.

The thirty-minute drive took forever. I got more and more tense with every red traffic light, as if by being late, we would miss our chance and you'd be gone.

Finally we arrived at a low, one-storey family home in suburbia, picket fence and green grass, sprinklers throwing rainbows over the front lawn. I grabbed your dad's hand walking up the path onto the porch. We rang the bell. A burst of activities: greetings, introductions, people talking, last-minute questions, forms to be filled in, phones ringing, and then silence.

We sat next to each other on a worn sofa, dust dancing in sunbeams, crisscrossing the room. At a right angle to us was another matching sofa; opposite, under the window, a big wooden desk with framed pictures, a vase with plastic flowers, and a smell of ink and dusty books reminding me of long-ago school rooms.

Were those baby noises I heard from next door? Were you already there?

The door opened and a procession of people filed in. First came a woman with kind brown eyes and the smallest bundle in her arms. Towering over her, like he was going to protect them against all evil, was a teddy bear of a man who appeared to be her husband, followed closely by two girls, maybe eight and ten years old, giggling behind busy fingers, playing with blonde ponytails. Last, our social worker and two other official looking women we had probably met earlier.

All of a sudden, there you were, in my arms. The unfamiliar feeling of a small human being against my body; tears welling up, your dad peeping over my shoulder; your new smell, like warm bread and soap bubbles; people explaining things; the kind lady who placed you in my arms giving us a small parcel in gift wrap.

The family, it turned out, was your kangaroo family, Kirsten and Tom and their two daughters, who had picked you up from the hospital two weeks previously and looked after you until this day. I was trying to be calm. As I looked down, a tear dropped onto your sleeping face.

Kirsten explained your routines and that you were such a "good baby". I wondered what that meant. You woke up, faraway eyes unfocused, and started crying. You had no tears yet, I was told. Those would come later. Somebody showed me how to change your nappy, how to swaddle you, how to support your neck and hold your bottle. In the midst of all of this, you fell asleep again, eyes shut against a world that had already proved itself unsafe for you to trust.

All my expectations of how this moment would transform me into the mother I was always meant to be crumbled with the flash of one thought: I had no idea what I was doing.

I also remember a vague feeling of surprised relief that you were placed with a white kangaroo family, just a shadow of a thought drifting in and out of my consciousness. It was far too early for me to realise that this was something worth noticing. I just sat there, stunned and overwhelmed, waiting for something to happen that would turn me into your mother.

On the drive home I sat in the back with you, holding on to the baby carrier like it was an explosive device that could go off with each swerve and stop of the car. You were still sleeping, barely visible under the pink fluffy blanket in which they'd wrapped you. I begged whoever would be listening up there that you wouldn't wake up again until we were home.

A series of firsts followed: my first nappy, my first bottle, my first evening alone in the house with you. Alan had gone out to celebrate his new dad status with some of his friends, the obligatory cigar was mentioned. Sitting by the pool under the night sky, I held the baby monitor on my lap, listening to the static, imagining I could hear you breathe. I remember thinking, "I am a mother now, and this is what it feels like," not sure what I was feeling. (Turned out I didn't need the monitor, for whenever you woke up, your unhappiness could be heard in every corner of the house and throughout the neighbourhood. For such a tiny person, you made a lot of noise.)

My first morning alone in the house with you.

You were finally asleep for some minutes between feedings and nappy changes, exhausted after yet another bout of seemingly endless and inconsolable crying. I wandered aimlessly around the house, lost in previously familiar rooms, the lone survivor of my inner tsunami sifting through the debris, trying to piece my life back together. Like you, I cried. I had no words for my sorrow, only blurred images and feelings so overwhelming they swallowed me whole.

When Alan came home to take over, I went to the shops, where I wandered around unfamiliar aisles, picking up a whole new language along with items like baby wipes, steriliser, and lactose-free formula that wouldn't make your tummy sore (one explanation for your endless crying). I was wondering how people could go about their daily business so unaffected when my whole world had just imploded. I felt out of control, and it surprised me that people didn't stop me, a confused looking woman wandering around a shopping centre, the snail marks of unwiped tears on her cheeks.

Coming home felt like landing in the middle of an accident scene. Things were strewn around everywhere; there were smells of warm milk, spilt body fluids and panic. Alan looked at me with red eyes, as shell-shocked as I felt. You cried your eerie tearless cry, the sound of a baby bird that had fallen out of its nest.

We took you into our bed, your impossibly tiny body dark between our pale limbs. They told us to lie together naked. It felt strange and invasive. I held you against my body like a ceramic doll, trying to breathe and be calm. I felt hopelessly inadequate.

"Do you think this is normal, her crying so much?" Alan asked me.

"I don't know. I don't even know what we were thinking. We can't do this, I can't do this." My tears were flowing again; I didn't even notice them anymore.

"Yes, we can," said your dad. "One moment at a time. We just do what needs to be done and all will be fine."

As I held you through our first nights and days, I wrapped these words around us like a life jacket keeping us afloat as waves of emotion kept crashing over us.

One moment at a time.

"All will be fine," I whispered against the silky petal of your ear, over and over again. "I know you are sad, I know you miss your mama, but I am here now, I will never leave you and I will love you. I know I will."

I don't think you believed me.

12

My Unlucky Brown Baby

We grew stronger, all of us together. Friends came to look at you while you were asleep. My mum visited from Germany, crying happy tears when she saw her first grandchild.

We took you on well-orchestrated outings, a walk along the beach, visits with family, lunch at nearby restaurants. People were supportive and happy for us.

Total strangers gazed into the baby carrier we took turns strapping to our chests, your little face always resting close to our hearts. They saw your fine black curls, your brown skin, and felt free to comment:

"Such a cute baby, where did you get her?"

"This is such a good thing you are doing!"

"Agh shame, so is she healthy?"

"So, could you not have your own?"

At first I felt confused. I struggled to understand how all these smiley comments, delivered with such kindness, made me want to lash out and hit people. It had never occurred to me to comment on a total stranger's baby or choice of conception. I guess I was never that interested in babies in the first place. But other people seemed to be. Babies clearly triggered some sort of collective need to express feelings and opinions that were utterly unasked for. The questions and comments made me feel raw and violated, and even though I knew you did not understand, I felt the urge to cover your ears and shield you from a new reality that was slowly shifting into focus: we were not normal.

By becoming your mother, I had slipped down the slope to abnormal, a white mother with a brown baby presumably acquired through adoption. Or maybe somewhere in the background there was a black man?

Does it seem silly to you that I had not thought this through before? Looking back, I see this new mother, and I cringe at her blue-eyed ineptness, her simplistic, one-dimensional understanding of a world that, until the day you came into her life, had mostly served her as the stage on which she could live out her every dream. Everything she did not achieve or see through to the end was her own choice, or simply not meant to be, just another opportunity to learn and grow.

So what if my baby had a different skin colour to mine? Why should that be important? I would raise you, protect you, teach you, and ultimately prove that race and skin colour were just a minor stumbling block on the way to self-realisation, which we could easily overcome by adjusting our mindset.

I took me a while to realise that this worldview was created on the basis of a massive blind spot, covered up by a rose-coloured patch I had never even noticed. But that was much later.

First, I became angry.

There was the time when we were invited to a family friend's house. As new parents, we were forever set up on blind dates with other parents.

"Oh, you must meet so-and-so. They are so lovely, just had their second baby, a little girl, about Lele's age. We are invited there for a braai on Sunday, why don't you come along?"

So we surrendered our previously antisocial stance and ventured into the new realm of baby-centred socialising. You were still sleeping most of the time, and conversations took on a hypnotic flow around baby formula, nappy contents and sleep routines.

It was a Sunday afternoon, unusually hot for autumn. People were gathered on deep-seated couches on a porch, piano music in the background, smells of freshly mown grass, expensive perfumes and clean babies. Sliding glass doors opened onto the lounge, cream-coloured curtains gently swaying in a breeze from the ocean.

I had stepped away from the chatter into the living room to change and feed you. The latter had become an exercise that required me dancing around in bouncy little steps so you would stay awake for the task and also be distracted from your determination not to allow food into your body. The doctor, whom I had called on an hourly basis days earlier – when I was convinced I was doing everything wrong and you would starve to death – had given me patient and futile advice, "Babies don't starve themselves, she is a healthy baby, and she will feed. Just keep on offering her the bottle." *Easy for him to say*, I thought, and, *he doesn't really know you*.

Maybe you were going to be the first baby to prove him wrong.

So I kept on trying out new positions, dance moves, and various songs until I eventually discovered that if I distracted you with the right amount of hopping and rocking, you took little sips, avidly following the merry-go-round of colourful couches, pictures and armchairs revolving around you. (Later on, I discovered the green bouncy ball, which became your regular feeding spot.)

As I was hopping about our new friend's living room, beautiful woven rugs and wall hangings swimming in and out of my line of vision, I suddenly had a floaty, slightly drunk feeling, as if I was standing still in the centre of the merry-go-round. I clung to you like you were my anchor in this moving sea and you opened your eyes and looked at me with such wisdom and understanding that I almost expected you to say something profound and life changing. I felt exposed and vulnerable in all my insecurity and imperfection, but also held and comforted at the same time, as if the whole universe was lovingly gazing at me through your eyes.

Then you looked away again with your unfocused gaze drifting somewhere beyond the room into a fairy world only you could see. I realised how tired I was.

As the world shifted back into focus, I found myself standing in front of a row of photographs depicting happy white people with happy white babies. I felt dizzy and nauseated and, looking for a place to sit, dropped onto the nearest couch, landing in the middle of a conversation.

"My friends also just adopted, they tried for years to have their own children, but they were getting too old and a few weeks ago they got a little boy." A woman in stylishly casual shorts, showing off her toned and tanned legs, French pedicure and matching flip-flops, pointed to one of the pictures: happy white couple with happy white baby.

Adopted? I wondered, but I quickly joined in with the collective cries of, "awww, how sweet" and "so precious" and "cute".

"Yes," said the woman, who I remembered was our hostess, in reply to the unasked question in the room, "They were lucky, they got a white baby."

I felt these words like a punch to my stomach. My breath left my body, leaving me deflated like a party balloon popped by a careless child. I must have pressed you against me too hard and you started crying, alerting everybody to my presence, and oh, how I just wanted to disappear into those fluffy cushions with my unlucky brown baby.

To my great surprise, nobody flinched or paused or even noticed us. The chatter carried on, inconsequential, brushing over the subject like somebody had mentioned the weather.

I sat there, holding you tight, your little bird cries muffled against my shoulder.

It was on that day, just after the moment of our first magical connection, that a crack appeared in my world. Suddenly I noticed people's comments about "them and us", comments I had so easily shrugged off before as nothing serious: just people having a vent, complaining about their black housekeepers stealing bread and toilet paper, or about the nanny sleeping in their beds while they were at work; party chatter about black people begging at traffic lights or loitering around our white neighbourhoods, posing a threat to our safety. In a neighbourhood meeting, it was decided that "we must cut down the trees and bushes in our streets, so we can see the undesirables".

In the park, somebody asked if I was taking you out for the day (*how nice of you*).

Then there were the jokes. People socialising around fires, grilling sausages and chicken, kids screaming nearby, while the parents were having a laugh about GMT versus BPT (Greenwich Mean Time or Black Peoples' Time). Or a joke about how to prevent black people from jumping on hotel beds (you tape Velcro to the ceiling). Sometimes I even heard myself laugh, felt my silent nod of agreement, before a stabbing feeling reached my insides and the reality sunk in, that they could have been speaking about your other mother or father, of whom I knew next to nothing.

And the gifts we received from friends and family: countless first baby books with little white fairies and little white princesses; dolls with silky blonde tresses; a white rabbit that could squeak; and even a white dog with a little golden bell attached to its collar. I felt ungrateful and on the verge of a mental illness that made me hypersensitive to white things. I saw it everywhere: the whiteness of my world swallowing you up like a cheese-coloured giant.

13

The Little Black Girl

I had a conversation with my friend B when you were about two. She was my only close friend in Cape Town back then. She had moved into our neighbourhood shortly after you were born.

From the moment I saw her driving down the road in her open top vintage car, laughing at something her five-year-old daughter had said, I wanted to be her friend. She was beautiful, but not in the sense that certain features put together create beauty. B's beauty was a mysterious combination of opposites. One moment it was there, obvious like a shiny red apple in a black-and-white movie; the next moment it was hidden behind the shadows in her face and the weight in her steps. She could be all glamour and giggles, a firework of artful metaphors and brilliant deductions, weaving outrageous stories from everyday boringness with her long fingers dancing exclamation marks to her punch lines. She became a neon rainbow spanning my horizon. Being around her felt like watching an awe-inspiring spectacle. We became friends, head over heels, barely taking a breath in nonstop talking marathons, unfolding each other's stories like bundles of colourful fabric.

Until something inevitably changed once more, like the tides of the ocean. Her features turned slack and drawn, pale eyes looking out from behind round spectacles, unsteady and weak.

For a long time, typical of a child of divorcing parents, I attributed this sudden change solely to my wrongs. I made a desperate show of my sulkiness, but I truly believed that if I just worked hard enough and proved myself sufficiently, I could win her back.

I always did win her back. It was nothing I did or didn't do, she would just come rolling back into my life when the time was right, like the incoming tide.

It was on one of our early Sunday morning walks, the sun barely up over the ocean. We were trotting along Sea Point promenade, arms swinging and words flying, dodging dogs, cyclists, and other early exercisers.

"So, this swimming teacher in Leila's class wants to show me this gadget one of the kids is using in the pool," B started her story. "He wants to point out the kid to me, who incidentally is the only black boy in the pool. He can't identify him by the clothes, clearly, 'cause they're all in the water, so he's umming and aahing and eventually comes out with, 'Umm, the little boy with the blue swimming cap', which is about half the kids in the pool, all the while stabbing a finger desperately in the direction of the black boy."

"What, seriously?" I laughed easily as we passed a couple of screeching gulls and a strangely dressed bearded guy sitting on a bench. He was mumbling to himself, arms and legs hidden in the depths of an old trench coat like an overstuffed teddy bear outlived by his grown-up childhood friend.

"Yeah, can you believe it? He was so shit scared to say 'black' that he grabbed at anything to avoid it, even if it was obvious."

"Umm, I might do that too sometimes." This surprised me as I was saying it.

"What do you mean?" She sidestepped a puddle of oily looking water with bits of styrofoam floating on the surface.

"Parents ask me at parties, so which one is yours, and

I say, 'the little girl in the pink tutu' instead of saying the little black girl, even if she's the only one there."

"Hmm, that's strange." B scanned me with a sideways glance that I was not quite ready to interpret.

We walked on in silence for the next kilometre or so. The sun was high now, reaching for the back of my neck, pinpricks of heat just under my skin. I didn't sweat, though; I just got hot and claustrophobic.

"If she were the only blonde girl in a room full of brown haired people, you would not hesitate for a second to refer to her as the little blonde girl, right?" she eventually continued her thread.

"No, I suppose I wouldn't."

"So why not say the little black girl?" There was an added sharpness to the careful pronunciation of the last two words.

"I don't know. It's as if it is a bad word in a way. And technically she is not black. Her skin is brown, right?" I paused for air. Taking in too much, I gasped. "Besides, her birth family is coloured." I almost tripped as we left the paved path and continued along a stretch of lawn. As I caught myself, she reached out and grabbed my arm. I pulled away, irritated with my stumbling and with her helpful presence.

"A bit too much information when you are asked which one is your kid, no?" She didn't let it go.

Another minute or so passed. We were back on the pavement. A wave crashed against the rocks below, splashing over the low wall and spraying us with salty rain. A dad on roller skates passed us with one of those trendy aerodynamic three-wheeler prams. The baby's plump fists clinging to the side bars, his face reminded me of a cartoon figure, like Tom or Jerry plummeting down a cliff, eyes big with the adrenalin rush, the mouth a perfect O, two front teeth peeping out under a blue sunhat with bunny ears.

"Well …" I was catching up to B's faster pace. "Surely

I shouldn't be deciding for her. If she wants to define as black or brown or coloured or none of that, that's up to her, right?"

"It's just skin colour, what's the big deal?" B was speeding up again, not bothered whether I was still in hearing distance.

"It's not that it's a big deal to *me*," I heard my defensive whine, "I just don't want to stereotype her as a black girl."

"But she is a black girl," she said, matter-of-factly.

"Well no, she is not!" I was racing ahead now, arms swinging like I was getting ready to throw a punch. "Her birth mum is coloured and, anyway, it should be her choice. What if a mixed-race kid decides she identifies more with her white heritage, why can't she call herself white?"

"Because she isn't." Quick and sharp.

I knew I was being baited like a fat stupid carp in a pond full of clever fish. I watched myself with grim satisfaction as I jumped in slow motion from the platform of sensible into the void of unreasonable, unhinged argumentative bitch, "So white is only the Aryan, fascist pure master race bullshit and everything else is black?"

"Whoa, I'm just saying, don't bite my head off!" B held out her arms, palms raised in mock surrender, scanning my face with her relentlessly bright eyes. I refused to look at her.

We walked in silence until we got back to the car.

"Call me."

"OK, bye."

I drove home in a fog of anger and confusion. Why was she not getting my point? What was my point? Why was I so angry?

14

Kal

Happiness runs in a circular motion,
life is like a little boat upon the sea;
everything is a part of everything anyway,
and you can have it all if you let yourself be.

This is a sweet little meditation I learned years ago on a yoga retreat. It has a childlike magic to it, and I used to sing it to you during the first few days of your life with us. This is about how you came to me, Kal, my strong and beautiful child, my little god of destruction, and about your special magic.

We had given our application to the adoption agency in late September, anticipating a comfortable waiting period of a couple of months, easing us into the idea of transitioning from a contented little threesome to a family of four. We expected you to arrive sometime in January or February the following year, a quiet time in our business after the Christmas rush. But you had other plans.

On the sixth of October 2008, a cool and sunny Monday morning, the phone in my office rang. I was greeted by E, our social worker, expecting her to ask when she could come for a house visit, or to tell us we needed to send in another reference or that a new form had to be signed. Instead she said, "I have your child here."

I sat down hard on my freewheeling office chair, nearly

missing the seat in front of my paper-strewn desk. I gestured at your dad, who happened to come into the room as I took the call, looking for some scribbled phone number amidst the chaos.

He looked up at me, shrugging his shoulders, palms up in a silent *What's up with you?*

"B a b y," I mouthed at him, with exaggerated lip movements, simulating a scream of teenage-girl-reality-TV proportions. Your dad stared at me, lips apart, breathing through his mouth. Feeling behind him with one arm, he grabbed the nearest chair and collapsed into it, his eyes bright with panic.

"I have to call you back," I interrupted E, whose soothing voice steadily continued over the whooshing sound in my ears.

"That's all right," she said. "You don't have to do it, if it's too early for you. I told the mum, you're not ready yet, but she insisted I ask you. So take your time, think about it first."

"We can't say no," I said to Alan as I put down the phone.

"No, I suppose we can't."

For a while we just looked at each other. Only a week ago, we had climbed up our "Wishing Dune" in Arniston, looking out over the ocean, breathing in the early morning breeze of fresh, salty air, the sky and the sand blending into a perfect aquarelle of greys and greens. We closed our eyes to send our silent wishes for you and everything else we desired on that day into the universe, and when I opened mine, just about to take the first leap off the steep incline, arms outstretched, screeching like a sea gull, feet sinking deep into the sand, I saw her. She leapt out of the waves, sending silver fountains into the sky, like waving a greeting our way. Then she was gone. As we were running down our "Wishing Dune" that day, we both knew that somehow you were connected to that magic whale and would be with us soon.

We had no idea just how soon.

As we reached the bottom of our dune, you were already waiting for us in the safe house where Joanna had dropped you off after deciding that she needed to share her journey as your mother. She had sat at the same table where, only hours before, we had left our profile box containing pictures and descriptions of each of us. Maybe absent minded, maybe made curious by the blue box decorated with paper flowers and bows, she must have opened it and looked through the contents while she was waiting for a social worker to talk to her.

"These are my baby's parents," she then told the person who came to speak to her.

They told her that the profile was not supposed to be there; that it hadn't been "processed" yet. They said we were not ready and that there were other people who had been waiting longer. But she only repeated what she knew, "These are my baby's parents. You need to ask them first."

The necessary wheels whirred and clicked into place, our profile was "processed", and two weeks later we got the call. "It would be like ignoring a sign from the universe that we know will make total sense one day; we just haven't understood it yet, right?" Your dad seemed shaky and a little surprised by his own words.

As was I. Normally, this would have been my line. I am usually the one enlisting the universe for all sorts of miracles while he is warily watching from the sidelines, ready to come to the rescue when it all goes wrong. So far he hasn't had to bring out his white horse and whisk me away from danger, but it warms my heart to know he is always ready. So when I heard him talk about signs from the universe, I felt a little disoriented, as if I was walking down a familiar road and discovered a garden full of exotic flowers I had never noticed before. I wondered if he might be in shock.

"Are you sure about this?" I asked him.

Then your dad said the most beautiful thing, "I am only sure about one thing, and that is when your heart speaks, I have learned to listen."

I reached across the desk and took his hand. We sat for a while, the familiar feel of our hands fitting together soothing the storm inside of me. There was joy and fear and urgency. So many things needed to be done, from bringing the Moses basket up from the garage and preparing your sleeping space, to buying nappies and formula and little warm things to wrap you in.

"You have to phone them back and tell them," your dad said.

"Yes." I felt a silly grin spread across my face. "That was quick. It has to be tomorrow," I said. I didn't want you to stay with strangers a moment longer than you had to.

"So call them now." Your dad didn't even hesitate.

I picked up the phone. And then it was done.

The next morning, after a day of preparations and stomach-churning excitement, we drove along the motorway to the meeting place outside a McDonald's drive-through. The social workers were waiting for us in their car to direct us to the safe house, where Joanna would be "doing the handover." The scene made me want to giggle, like we were actors in a spy comedy. Following a lollipop red Golf, we ignored stop streets, cut in front of other cars, and even sped through a traffic light about to turn red. I wondered if the woman in the backseat of the Golf with the blonde braid extensions might be your mother and asked Alan to go faster so I could get a closer look.

Finally, the Golf turned into the driveway of an unremarkable two-storey house in a street with orderly trees and square lawns. We parked on the side of the road opposite the driveway and joined the three women on the steps to the front door. We shook hands. There was E, our social worker, S, Joanna's social worker, and Joanna, the woman with the blonde braids. Her handshake was soft and light like a child's. E rang the doorbell. I could hear the ding-dong resonating somewhere in the depths of the house. Nobody even attempted to make small talk while we waited to be admitted, a complicated procedure involving an intercom and a trellis door with an attitude. Eventually we all filed into a serious lounge: ornate wooden furniture, old-fashioned upholstery with floral patterns, and heavy damask curtains submerging the room in a devout darkness. There were religious quotes on the walls and family pictures in silver frames on a sideboard. It smelled of furniture polish and hospital food.

We all sat down. I sank next to Alan into one of the frilly sofas, the three women with Joanna in the middle took a seat on the other sofa at a right angle to us. There was a plastic folder on the coffee table between us with the adoption agency's logo and a baby picture on the cover. I knew this must be you, but it was too gloomy to see anything clearly.

The social workers introduced us properly and S talked on behalf of Joanna, whom she said was too emotional to speak. We got told her age, background, and the reason she wanted us to be your parents.

"Joanna wants baby to have a better life with two parents and a sibling," S finished her recital as if reading from a file.

I tried not to stare at your mother, wondering if you would have her bright sparkly eyes that seemed to hide a naughty giggle, or maybe her small symmetrical mouth, lips touching lightly like two soft pillows.

They all looked at me expectantly and I realised I had been asked a question which still lingered like an echo in the room, "Do you have any questions for Joanna?"

We looked at each other then, your two mums. I had no idea what to say. Then, just as I was about to ask, she said to me in a surprisingly strong voice, "Don't worry, I won't change my mind."

Then she got up. I stood up too, not sure if I was meant to go with her. Somebody entered the room with a camera and suggested this was a good moment to take pictures: two mothers embracing. So we hugged each other awkwardly, her head at the height of my chest, her arms limp around my waist. I felt big and oppressive towering over her. Then she pushed away from me and headed to the stairs leading to the upper floor where the babies were kept.

Moments later she came down again with a small bundle in her arms. You were sleeping, a drop of milk glistening between the two perfect pillows of your lips. As she put you in my arms, I could feel the tears that I had so far managed to hold back spill out of my eyes.

"Are you sure?" I whispered to Joanna. She smiled at me through her own tears.

"Don't worry Martina, this is what I want for my child."

Then you opened your eyes.

I will never forget that moment. You looked at me with calm focus, not afraid of eye contact, like only very young children or yogis, or my therapist back in Berlin, are capable of. There was confidence and knowing in your sparkly eyes. A tear dropped from my chin onto your cheek, and I was taken back to when I first held Lele. With Lele I was overwhelmed by the magnitude of our new relationship and the fact that within the blink of an eye I had become responsible for a helpless little person. With you, I was afraid that I might not live up to the mother you were about to lose. But even more than that, I was in awe of your presence. Holding you this first time felt like sitting on a rock surrounded by the ocean. Everything about you was alive and moving with a natural energy that was deeply connected to an all-knowing wisdom.

With your eyes you were simply saying, "I am here."

As soon as we brought you home, I was bogged down by a vicious virus, unable to eat or get up or even talk without feeling dizzy and nauseous.

Lying in my bed helplessly, I quickly surrendered to the firm grip of Guilt and her little sister Regret.

What had I done? How could I have thought I was cut out to be your mother? What was I doing to your sister, who had been the centre of my universe for the last thirty months and still needed me so much, and was too small to understand that this little stranger taking her place was her new sibling and part of our family?

Above all, I felt guilty for not loving you enough, without realising that I had been there before, and that love couldn't reveal itself if my heart was filled with fear and my mind blocked by expectations.

During all this time – I think it was almost a week of physical and emotional purging – you were the one who stayed calm and grounded, and whenever I stuck my nose out from under my duvet, you reminded me that no matter how long it would take me to come out of my self-induced drama and join you on the adventure that would be our life together, you'd be there, waiting for me to catch up. You became my teacher then, a three-month-old baby, teaching me about trust and – once again – love. I still feel a pinch of regret that I was not able to be fully present and appreciate the magic that brought you to us, the magic that is you.

I think you know me well enough by now to realise I don't do change very well or in the least bit gracefully. Instead I turn into a mixture of drama queen and posttraumatic stress victim, barely able to look beyond these first moments of upheaval that are the inroads into my new life. Of course, change is in the nature of each parenting journey. So there have been and still are plenty of moments when I am faced with the challenges of my emotional handicap. Sometimes you look at me in the midst of a mothering meltdown, and ask in your calm voice of reason, "Mama, do you need a hug?"

"Thank you, darling, that would be so nice." The comfort of your strong arms around me, from when they could barely reach around my neck to when they now slip easily around my waist, is like coming home to myself all over again.

Thinking about our first weeks together, I have one picture in my mind: you were propped up like a little Buddha in your Moses basket, outside on our veranda, surrounded by friends and family, all the new people in your life who came to look at you. I was standing a couple of metres away, ready to jump in if it should get too much for you, but you just sat there, calmly observing. You didn't smile or engage with anybody just because they were there. Instead you seemed to think about it first and then decide whether to make the required effort to connect with a person in front of you, or rather stay in meditative rest. Whenever you did decide to smile and acknowledge somebody's presence, they walked away feeling special and honoured. Mostly you chose to quietly contemplate people instead of engaging with them.

When I look into your sparkly eyes today, I see the glimmer of determined mischief or abundant happiness or pure anger or whatever emotion is consuming you at the time, and my heart does one big leap with my love for you. You became my teacher at three months old; you continue to teach me every day. With Lele, I learned that I could be a mother. You remind me every day to be the best mother I can be.

15

Nene

I need to speak to you about my health, Martina.

Squinting at the screen of my phone, eyes barely open, I had no idea what that message was about to set in motion. It entered our living room at the tail end of a benign movie-watching-stretched-out-on-the-couch-after-the-kids-are-asleep-Sunday, like a half-forgotten friend who drops in unannounced for a glass of wine before informing us that he is going to move in for good.

The text was from Joanna, Kal's first mum, with whom I had kept in touch against the advice of our social workers and the stipulations of some law I chose to know nothing about. We had met up a few times, negotiating the awkwardness of our single-stranded connection with nervous chatter about first words, tooth fairies and Easter bunnies, all the while measuring each other with hopeful trepidation out of the corners of our eyes. Sometimes we were lost for words.

The first time we had seen each other again, a few years after the "handing over", she still looked like I remembered her: soft, like a friendly cloud in a storybook. When our eyes met, I instantly melted into the familiar glimmer of Kal's ready laughter. There was a spark of mischief over something broken, like a gilt glaze over cracked china.

I hugged her close, imagining my grown child in my arms. We sat down next to each other on a chipped wooden bench under autumn trees, the soft breeze around us carrying smells of freshly mown grass and her flowery perfume, cut ever so often by the whiff of a dog relieving itself nearby. This being a "good" neighbourhood, inevitably the owner would come strolling along, bag the offending pile and amble off again, face set in neutral-alert as if to challenge anyone who might suspect him of neglecting his dog-owner duty or who might question the sanity of people proudly walking around with plastic bags of excrement swinging from their wrists.

I thought I could sense in her a hidden amusement at the shenanigans of white folk having nothing better to do than stroll in a park at midday picking up after their dogs.

Of course we didn't speak about that.

"Tell me about Kal," she said instead, refocusing her bright gaze on the space above my head.

"He is so grown up already, always telling us exactly who or what he wants to be and what he needs us to do about it," I told her, pausing for her reaction.

"Really?" Her hand flew to her mouth as if to stop more words from spilling out.

"Yes, he told us a week before his third birthday, he was done with Barney and all things purple or too "girlish" looking, so we had to buy new outfits and change the birthday cake from Barney to Spiderman. Here is a picture of him on his birthday, he was wearing his new Spiderman pyjamas all day." I needed to take a breath and let her scroll through the pictures on my phone, our heads close together like friends.

Her giggle was so familiar.

"Wow, Martina, how do you deal with that?"

"I think it's great, him knowing his own mind so well."

"He's clever," Joanna added.

"Yes."

There was a splash from the fountain a few metres away where two big black dogs had landed in the water, panting their pink tongues at each other, faces ridiculously happy.

"You know, Martina, I never bonded with Kal." I could barely hear her above the splashing and barking.

"You did what you could."

"You know Kal's dad left me when I was pregnant." Her fingers kneaded my phone in her lap. She had beautiful hands, like Kal. I wanted to say something soothing, take the sting out of her words.

"You had a hard time back then," was all I could come up with. My voice sounded like an echo, weak and distant.

"I fell in love with his uniform, you know, he was in the army." There it was again, the spark of mischief lighting up her whole face.

"Yes, you told me. Are you still in touch?" I wondered how Kal would one day feel about this distant figure of a father who didn't want anything to do with a child and abandoned his mother because of him.

"No, I never see him." She handed me my phone, reached into the brown bag resting open-mouthed between us, and pulled out her BlackBerry. After a few clicks she angled it towards me so I could see the baby picture.

"Wow, is that Kal?" I was touched that she would have kept a picture of our child on her phone.

"No, Martina, that is Nene, his sister."

I knew she had had another child a few months before, a planned pregnancy this time and what she called her last chance at motherhood. She once again chose a man in uniform (the giggle again) but was not going to fall in love. She didn't want him in her life. This time around, she wanted her own child and she was going to get it right, she assured both of us. My initial worries (or were they hopes?) that she might ask me to take the baby eased as the months went by. I managed to avoid thinking about Kal's little sister and what it would mean for all of us to know that she existed.

Seeing the picture that day, a little copy of my own child, was shocking. I noticed that I was holding my breath and I let it out – deliberately and slowly – so it wouldn't seem like I was gasping at the sight of her.

"She is the light of my life," Joanna said, lips softly parted, eyes shining.

I felt a stab of jealousy for my child, her other child, whom she could not love. But I said, "That is so beautiful. I am happy for you."

"Thank you." She said it gravely, as if I had extended my condolences. "You know, I really bonded with her; it is totally different this time. I really love her."

"You loved Kal too," I reminded her, a little too abruptly.

"Yes of course I do. But this is different. I felt so bad about Kal. I was a bad mother I think." She gripped her hands tightly, her eyes cloudy with held back tears.

"No, you were not. You had a hard time, you were sick and alone. You walked all the way to Paarl with a baby in your arms so you could take your child to a safe place." I could feel my face heating up. I was talking a little too loud, as if trying to convince her of something we both needed to believe.

I also knew I was right. I knew this as I knew of my own love, which I had to dig out from under layers of lies and misconceptions about motherhood, like pulling a breathing thing from a grave of unyielding earth.

"Yes, that is true." She sighed and hugged herself, a shiver brushing her body. The sky had turned dark, a wall of clouds blocking out the afternoon sun. A gust of wind blew a pile of swept-up leaves along the path, some of them clinging to our legs as we both got up simultaneously, as if an invisible bell had called an end to our meeting. We both started talking.

"I should go now," she said.

"I need to get the kids," I said.

"Thank you for meeting me, Martina, it means a lot to me."

"Thank you for coming," I said, "I am so glad I found you again."

When we hugged this time, she gripped me a little tighter. There was so much more I wanted to say, so much I wanted to know. I had a sense of time slipping away from me, as if this could have been my one chance to get something right and now it was over.

We took a selfie for Kal, arm in arm in front of a tree. Her head barely reached my shoulder. Later I noticed how our smiles were alike, soft and gentle, like we were secretly watching a child we both loved playing with his toys and talking to himself.

As I walked back to my car that day, after our first post-adoption meeting, I felt relieved that I could like her, maybe even love her. I had been doubting my own instincts, worried by stories from well-meaning strangers warning me of the dangers of birth mothers taking advantage and enmeshing themselves into an adoptive family's life. A wrong move, I was told, could damage my children and threaten our happily-ever-after.

When Joanna contacted me on that Sunday evening a few weeks before Christmas, saying she needed to talk to me about her health, I didn't have an immediate premonition. She had recently moved to Johannesburg and we had ex-changed many texts over the last few months. She would ask for pictures of Kal or my advice about what to give her baby for a cough or an upset tummy. We were talking about meeting up with the children someday so that Kal could meet them both. So far I had no buy-in from Kal, who told me (so wise for his four years) that he wasn't ready and that he wasn't interested in another mama, and that was the end of that.

Are you sick? I texted back, not bothering to rouse Alan from his half-slumber on the other couch.

Yes, it is serious, appeared the prompt answer, *I didn't want to tell you before, but the reason I moved to Johannesburg was that people in Cape Town knew I had HIV and I couldn't get a job.*

I felt like I had swallowed a rock.

"Put that on pause," I snapped at Alan, pointing to the remote on his chest.

He stared at me, disoriented, "What's going on?"

"Put that off," I repeated, a tinge of hysteria in my voice, "Joanna just texted me." I looked at my phone, texting her back, *So sorry to hear … are you OK?*

"OK, what is it, what does she want?" He said it in that deliberately soothing way, like he was speaking to an overexcited child. It was supposed to alert me to the fact that I was probably overreacting. It did nothing to calm me. It never does.

I am fine now, Martina, but I have been really sick with pneumonia for a few weeks. I am taking the drugs now and am a lot better.

"I think she wants us to take the baby," I said.

Alan sat up at that. "What?"

Do you need anything? I texted.

"You're not serious," his voice a pitch higher than normal.

"Well, let's see what she wants," I mocked his soothing tone, deliberately not looking up from my phone where her reply appeared. *I am fine – but I will have to take Nene to a home. It's too much for me with a toddler, she's walking now. When I was sick, it was all too much. I have to think of her future, when I won't be there.*

"She says she can't look after her anymore," I summarised for Alan.

You can live a long and healthy life, I patronised her in my panic, adding, *but we'll be there for her, if anything should happen to you*.

"Hold on." Alan was wide awake now, jumping onto the couch next to me, grabbing my hand with the phone. "What are you saying to her? We need to talk about this."

"Of course we will talk; I am not just going to say fine, we'll take the baby, without talking to you." I was too distracted to sound convincing. Alan could hear it too.

Are you serious, Martina? Will you take her? Joanna texted back.

She can't go to a home, I wrote, *If we can't help you to keep her, of course we'll take her.*

"I just said we'll take her." I looked up from my phone. For a moment we stared at each other, our panic perfectly mirrored in each other's eyes. Then we burst out laughing.

"Of course you did," he said.

We knew that night that you would come to us. Whatever our previous plans had been, whatever obstacles, real or imagined, might have prevented us from becoming your parents, it all faded into insignificance with one question: what could we possibly tell Kal on the day when he would ask us where his sister was and why we hadn't taken care of her? That we had other plans? That we were too old? That we only ever wanted two children?

There was really no choice for any of us. We might not have known this earlier, but we were always on a trajectory catapulting us into each other's lives. We just hadn't seen it coming.

Days went by in a blur. I remember talking to Joanna the next morning, abandoning my full trolley of weekly grocery shopping in an aisle and rushing out of the shop as soon as I saw her name on my screen. I sat down, feeling light-headed and unreal, as if I were merely an observer and it was somebody else making life-changing decisions while perched on a bench outside Woolworths with a mad rush of tourists and Christmas shoppers streaming past.

I recognised in Joanna's voice the determination I had seen in her eyes before, dampened at times by tears or laughter or insecurities, but nonetheless as strong and clear as the sudden bark of a foghorn demanding course corrections and making me jump as I walk past.

My jumpiness had nothing to do with the message and everything to do with the unexpectedness of it all. Everyone we knew was weighing in with their opinions, the general consensus being that we should hold off, let the social workers convince her to keep her child, or, if all else failed, find another suitable family and hope for the best.

What nobody said but many (including our social workers) thought was, *you knew it was a bad idea to contact the birth mother, but you wouldn't listen; now see what you have landed yourself in?*

16

Between Mothers

Joanna kept us all on course. "I know what I am doing. I won't change my mind. It's not about money; I can't be there for her the way she needs me. I realised when I was sick that I can't do this. I want you to be her mama and Kal and Lele to be her siblings. This is what is best for her," she told me on my bench outside Woolworths.

Two weeks later, she travelled to Cape Town with you and handed you over to the social workers, who took you to a place of safety. We were not allowed to be that. We were allowed to visit you. Sixty days, they told us. Two months during which Joanna would have to live in a separate safe house for birth mothers and work with a counsellor, with the ultimate goal that she would change her mind. Our society was not ready to accept motherhood as a transient journey that can be shared and divided and shaped – and should never be prescribed. Two months in limbo, a lifetime for you, a strange time of ups and downs for all of us.

We were told we might not be able to adopt you because your biological father had refused his consent. He had never before offered any support or even asked to meet you. Yet, for reasons only he would know, he wanted you to live with his mother. Joanna refused, "I would never see my child again. He is just doing this to punish me," and said she'd take you back. We were at an impasse.

Our social worker said to leave it up to her; she was going to talk to him again. Eventually she succeeded. In the meantime you had arrived at your foster home in a town close to McGregor, where we spent New Year's at Alan's mom – your grandma Su's – house. I saw that as a good sign.

We were allowed to visit you on New Year's Day, three days after you had arrived in your interim home. I was told not to expect too much, as you were still "adjusting to the new environment". You were hitting and biting, crying for your mama, and not allowing any white staff near you. They told me you were less anxious around black carers.

We left your siblings at the house with the two families who had come on holiday with us. Lele and Kal were excited and couldn't wait to have you home. Kal put his fluffy zebra in my bag to give to you so you wouldn't feel lonely after we left.

I, on the other hand, sank into utter despair, wondering if this had all been one big mistake: how could I ever replace your mama and what was I thinking, throwing a traumatised eighteen-month-old child into the volatile mix that is our family? I asked Alan to take the long way around and avoid the bumpy dirt roads so I wouldn't throw up in the car.

"Don't worry," he said. "All will be fine, she'll come to us soon."

I didn't have the the energy to unload my jumble of doubts, so I touched his cheek with my cold hand and mumbled something like, "I know."

Then, silently, I did something I hadn't done since I was a child of seven. I comforted myself with fantasies of golden-haired angels and a white-bearded God looking out for me from a fluffy cloud. I prayed to the angels, the universe, and to any entity who was willing to listen.

I prayed for a sign that I was doing the right thing.

I prayed for my confidence to come back to me.

I prayed that when we drove back on that same road, I would be sure again.

But I was not very hopeful.

We parked outside a featureless family home behind a white picket fence, disturbing the silence with the double slamming of our doors. As soon as I stepped out of the air-conditioned car, I felt my skin itch and my head swim with the onslaught of the midmorning desert heat. A signboard with something devout in Afrikaans indicated that we'd found the right place.

We rang the doorbell and got buzzed into a courtyard extending into a sloping garden, a jungle gym and blow up swimming pool between the main house on the right and a low building on the left that looked like a converted garage. There were baby noises coming from the left so we turned towards the low building, negotiated a child gate with a tricky mechanism, and eventually opened the glass door to a low-ceilinged room smelling of soap, disinfectant, and something sweet like milk and bananas.

The air was cool and I instantly felt more present and alert. There were 15 or so cots lined up along the sides of the room with a large shelf in the middle doubling up as storage and changing station. Two women were sitting on chairs near the entrance, bottle feeding babies, and another two or three were bustling about changing more babies, packing away clothes or preparing formula in the open kitchen unit opposite the entrance. The whining, gurgling, babbling and wailing, together with the chatting, laughing and soothing against the backdrop of a drama unfolding on the TV formed a hum not unlike an orchestra tuning their instruments before a performance. Everyone, except the babies, looked at us as we came in and greeted us with smiles and Afrikaans words I didn't understand. I said hello. Alan introduced us and started a conversation that soon faded into the other noises.

I saw you as soon as my eyes adjusted from the bright sunshine of the outside world to the twilight of the room. You sat on a blanket on the floor between the entrance and the little kitchenette, looking at something only you could see. You were wearing a pink top with sparkly writing over yellow and pink dotted shorts. Someone had styled your hair into eight fluffy pompons tied with multi-coloured rubber bands. I recognised you from the pictures Joanna sent me, but also because you were the only toddler in a room full of babies. There was a baby boy (dressed in blue) lying on his back under a mobile of stuffed animals next to you and another one (also in blue) squirming on his tummy, trying to keep his bobbing head up and reach for you at the same time.

The babies seemed to neither interest nor annoy you. You ignored them with persistent calm, holding onto a pink plastic toy phone with both hands, eyes still focused on the nearest corner next to the entrance. I sat down a little away from you on the floor.

You didn't turn your head, but in the slight stiffening of your body I could see that you had noticed me and were alert to what I might do. I didn't move from where I was sitting. My arms felt empty by my side. You looked so small and fragile and defiant of the entire world. I wanted to scoop you up and hold you close.

Instead I talked to you in a voice I used with Kal and Lele at bedtime, when I wanted them to go to sleep.

"Hi Nene, I am here to visit you."

You didn't acknowledge me, eyes firmly focused on your corner.

"Do you think you might want to show me the garden, we could go for a walk maybe?" Still nothing. At least you were not screaming and running away from me.

Out of the corner of my eye, I noticed Alan talking to a white woman who must have come into the room after us.

I could hear them speaking English, and I recognised the voice of the woman I spoke to earlier on the phone. I got up and held out my hand to her, "Hi, you must be Ilse, I am Martina, we spoke earlier. Thank you so much for allowing us to come today."

She looked tired. A straight black bob framing her open face and two dark smudges under her eyes made her look pale. "So nice to meet you, you're always welcome." She took my hand, her smile lighting up her whole face, and looked in your direction. "Have you met Nene then?"

As I was about to reply, you got up from the floor and without looking at anybody walked straight out the door. At the little gate, you stopped, making complaining noises, which were met by cheerful laughter from one of the carers, "Aai, you want to go outside, clever girl."

"She understands and has started to speak Afrikaans," Ilse explained. "They have taught her to say *outside*."

I felt a renewed stab of anxiety at our so utterly different worlds and the seemingly impossible task of connecting with you on any level. I wanted to get away from it all, overwhelmed and fearful, like I imagined you must have felt, and so I followed you outside. I opened the gate for you and walked a little behind you along the path towards the jungle gym. You stood for a while contemplating the slide and I sat down on a little wall close enough to touch you. "Do you want to go up the slide, should I help you?"

Predictably you didn't answer or look at me. But you didn't seem to mind my following you and for the moment that was good enough for me. You had turned away from the slide and had taken a few steps back towards the nursery when the dog started barking.

Your whole body reacted to that noise, tensing and crouching as if getting ready to sprint or jump. At the same time, your face crunched and folded into a mask of fear and misery. You turned towards me and leaped into my arms.

I caught you without thinking.

Your arms came around my neck and your warm face pressed against the top of my chest, your pompons tickling my chin. I didn't dare move. My world had shrunk to the sensation of your skin on mine. I held you tight, as I held my breath, held my feelings, and held my body in utter stillness. Then, slowly, I swayed from side to side, a blade of grass in the wind, and I whispered a made up song in your ear. I sang about you and me and Kal and Lele and Papa, the first German words that came to me. I sang about our becoming a family and your coming home soon. Your arms were gripping onto me as if it were only by the strength of your own effort that you could keep yourself safe, as if letting go would mean falling with nowhere to land.

I carried on singing and rocking until my arms grew heavy and my body started aching for a place to sit. And then I sang some more, until I could feel the grip around my neck relax. One little arm came tumbling down and your breathing changed.

You were fast asleep.

As you let go, something inside of me loosened and softened, and all my fears and insecurities dissolved in one big wave of gratitude and love, a love for nothing less but life itself that had brought me to this moment.

As I carried you in, people were surrounding us, exclaiming and smiling. Somebody took a picture. Through a fog of tears, I could see your dad looking at me across the room and I smiled as I recognised the moment when I held my child for the first time.

On the drive home, I felt calm and washed out. We didn't speak much. I wanted to hold onto the feeling for as long as I could, the feeling of being exactly where I was meant to be, the sense of knowing, the glimpse of an understanding of the perfection that is each moment. I felt serene like a Tibetan monk.

Of course that glimpse into enlightenment faded the moment we arrived back to a house full of questions and a whole life to reorganise.

18

Family of Five

It took another 41 days before we were allowed to bring you home. Meetings with social workers, a court appearance and more psychological screenings were the required hoops we had to jump through first. A psychologist sat us (two hours each) in front of a computer program where we had to once again click hundreds of questions, taking me back to our first "screening" almost a decade ago. Only this time I was alone in the room, and there were no jokes and laughs with your dad to lighten up the somber atmosphere of an interrogation. I had also forgotten my glasses and squinted at the screen with a borrowed pair from one of the secretaries at the psychologist's office. When we were done, the computer spat out a red flag. "I am a little concerned about your relationship." The psychologist, sitting opposite us in her consulting room, frowned at a stack of printouts and then smiled at us an apology and a question. Alan and I looked at each other not sure whether to laugh or be alarmed.

"What?"

"From your answers Martina, it appears that you don't have a strong bond with your partner."

"What?" I asked again, confused now, "Where did I say this?"

"Here in this section where the quality of your relationships is evaluated, you seem to rely strongly on a third person but not on your partner." She waved a piece of paper at us and then shuffled more pages around, looking for answers hidden amongst the printed paragraphs. Alan and I stared at her, worried now. After a few minutes, she looked up again.

"Here it is: All the questions about your relationship have negative answers."

"But this is impossible," I protested, "Wouldn't I know if I felt this way or had given answers to that effect?" I tried to keep the sarcasm out of my voice.

"Hmm, let me see what it says in the evaluation part here."

A few more minutes passed. Alan and I rolled eyes at each other.

Eventually she read this out to us, "It says here: *if the respondent doesn't answer a question, a negative answer is automatically assigned.* Looking at your questionnaire printout here, it seems you didn't reply to any of the questions about your relationship."

It turned out that I had skipped a few pages and, barely able to make out the words on the screen, had replied to the friendship questions as if those were the questions about my relationship. Relieved laughs all around. Then we were declared once again fit to be parents.

On our way to get you, we stopped over at the little farm in McGregor. Your foster mama thought it would be better for you if we didn't pick you up at the end of the day, but rather early the next morning. I suspected she found it hard to say goodbye to you and I was thankful for this breathing time before the next chapter in our lives. Lele and Kal were at home with Sam, our au pair, which left us with nothing to do but enjoy a quiet last supper before another home-coming.

We sat in the village's only restaurant, a candle and pizza between us.

I couldn't eat.

My insides were knotted and buzzing with my many

fears. There was the usual will-I-be-able-to-love-you hum interspersed with the occasional shrill note of this-is-the-biggest-mistake-of-my-life, steadily accompanied by the double drumbeat of I-can't-do-this and I-will-never-be-good-enough. Alan's face showed the helpless worry of a child whose home is regularly rattled by earthquakes and who realises for the first time that the foundations might after all not be strong enough to hold the walls together.

His doubts concerned me more than my own. I felt guilty, too. (*I should be stronger by now. After all, this was my idea.*)

Even though we had visited you twice a week over the last month and a bit, we were still strangers to you. At every meeting, we had to pick up the pieces all over again. It seemed that rather than strengthening our connection with each visit, we were slowly losing you to the many volunteers, rotating staff, visiting students and social workers all showering you (the only toddler in a room full of babies) with good intentions and random affections, but only teaching you not to trust the permanence of people or places or love.

Our timed visits could in no way compete with the steady presence of Ilse, who fought a losing battle trying not to become too attached, and who fell more in love with you each day as you learned to make your way up the stairs to her private quarters and refused to settle for anything less than her full-time attention.

You knew what you needed was a mother, not a team, and so you looked for her from the moment you opened your eyes in the morning. Alan and I were merely two extras on the stage of your life. Often our meetings started well enough with a little play and a few cautious hugs, but the moment Ilse appeared on the stairs or you heard her voice from inside the main house, you pinched and bit and fought your way out of my arms to pursue your single-minded determination to find her. I felt like a predator trying to lure a toddler away from the people she loves. After a while, Ilse left the house before we came to visit so you would "get used to us".

So when we were on our way to fetch you, I knew Ilse had already said her goodbyes and would not be at home. The drive was as familiar as a morning school run by now. Without me having to ask, Alan accommodated my nervous stomach by taking the long way. We travelled on tarred roads stretching towards a horizon flickering under the sun like the blue in a flame. Fields of irrigated greens, olive orchards and fruit farms swam along the periphery of my vision like bold streaks of finger-paint.

We didn't talk much, except to rehearse our exit strategy like we were planning an abduction. *We'll take her and leave as soon as we can, don't start chatting to the carers, you strap her in, I'll start the car, if she starts crying, have her dummy and a bottle ready …* I had visions of forcing a screaming child into the restraints of the car seat or having to hold her while she would pinch and bite to get back to her foster mama.

Instead of leaving the car opposite the house in the shade of a tree, as we did on our previous visits, we drove all the way to the gate this time and parked in front of the double garage for a quick getaway.

The buzzer sounded almost as soon as we rang the bell. One of the carers was waiting for us at the door, holding you in her arms, a sense of urgency in the air. We barely greeted each other. Another woman handed Alan a cardboard container, no bigger than a shoebox, with your few belongings. To me, she held out a bottle of warm milk and a blue plastic dummy. One of the babies started wailing inside, followed by laughter and loud, cheerful voices. You looked through us without any visible emotion. Your eyes reminded me of an unlit paper lantern, waiting for the spark within to bring the colours and shapes back to life.

Somebody had plaited your hair with white silky ribbons. I held out my arms and you came from one set of arms into mine like in a choreographed dance.

We said our thank-yous and waved goodbye, and before you could react or protest, you were strapped into Lele's old car seat and we were on our way.

The drive back was long and tense. You started crying ten minutes into the journey and didn't stop. I sat in the back with you, offering milk and dummies, holding your hand and wiping your tears and mine. I could see Alan looking at us in the rear-view mirror, a teardrop suspended at the end of his nose. As we turned into our road, you fell asleep. We sat in the car outside our house a few deep breaths longer and then our life together began.

You wandered around your new space like a lost duckling, always close to one of us, looking at everything and nothing with your big faraway eyes. Your siblings swirled around you like goldfish in a pond at feeding time, feverish with excitement; they swung back and forth between showering you with love and attention and resenting you for taking up space in my arms or on my lap.

That night, when everybody was finally asleep, I stood by your cot in the little guest room I had made up for you and listened to the sound of your breathing and the unfamiliar sleeping noises you made, like learning the melody to a new song. The landscape of your face, still so unfamiliar: from the feathery curve of your brows, to the long lashes on your cheeks, to the tip of your nose twitching in a dream or from a memory, to the pink curve of your lips, that I couldn't help but brush with the tip of my fingers. You stirred at my touch, your hands flying to your face, and you turned your body away from me. I stood for a while longer, my hand resting against your back, willing you to carry on sleeping, until your breathing deepened again.

Like a miracle, everybody slept until the morning.

Your papa took your siblings to school and then we were alone in the house. You followed me into the bathroom and stretched out your arms to be picked up. So I took you in the shower with me, your face against my neck, your fingers learning the feel of my skin. Afterwards I wrapped us both in my towelling gown and sat with you in my arms in front of the bathroom mirror. The white ribbons in your tightly braided hair were soggy and frayed. The forced perfection of your hairstyle disturbed me, as if there were an unwanted message in it, somebody's attempt to make your "otherness" to me, the white lady, more digestible. Or maybe it was just a pretty style for a special occasion. It didn't occur to me at the time that there might be another message in the loving care someone had put into styling your hair, knowing you'd be going to a white home. Demonstrating the knowledge and skills handed down from generations of black mothers, they sent me a subtle reminder, an expectation implied in raising a black child that I hadn't grasped yet.

Still holding you tight against me and without looking at what I was doing, my fingers started playing with your hair at first and then, one by one, I untied the ribbons, slowly untangling each braid, pausing ever so often to negotiate a knot or follow a different direction. You buried your face deeper into my gown and after a few minutes I felt your body relax and you fell asleep.

Your papa found us still in the bathroom when he came home midmorning (*you didn't answer your phone*) to check on us. I had just brushed out the last tangles with my fingers and admired your brand-new baby afro in the mirror when he tiptoed in, smiling and blowing kisses at our reflections.

You woke up and we dressed and started the day all over again.

The next three or four days dreamily flowed into each

other like that. Each morning, after everybody had left the house, I followed your script. Mostly you wanted to be as close to me as possible, your arms wound tight around my neck, your little face pressed into the skin of my arm or shoulder. We spent the morning outside on blankets in the sun, or on a daybed in the shade of the patio. Sometimes we moved inside onto a sofa or a bed. You usually fell asleep around 11 for an hour or two, while I read or did nothing, except for holding you. We didn't get up again until midday when it was time for your lunch.

At bedtime I sat with you until you were asleep and your siblings enjoyed extra TV time and your papa's attention before we could resume our previous sleep-time routine of songs and stories.

I couldn't believe it should all be so easy and the ever-anxious or maybe the wiser part in me waited for the storm to break. Your eyes were still distant and your smile had not returned. Rather than a relaxing into new routines, these first few days felt more like a holding of breath, like we were all waiting for something that would shake us into place so we could exhale and be new.

It only took a few days.

19

The Earth Shakes

It was Friday evening just after bath time. You had been with us for four days. As it was a weekend, your siblings were allowed to watch an entire movie and, for the hundredth time, they chose "air-pig" (*Epic*).

We were in my room after your bath and you rolled around on my yoga sheepskin as I was trying to massage you with lavender scented coconut oil. You were not used to massages and made a game out of slipping out of my fingers and crawling away, until I caught you again. There was a sense of mischief like you were on the verge of a giggle, but your eyes were unfocused and your emotions hidden deep within.

After another roll and wiggle, you rested for a moment flat on your back, hands by your side, your fingers playing with the wool of the sheepskin, your head tilted to one side, watching the shadow-play of leaves in the fading light outside my window. I could hear the cockroach people attacking the beautiful queen in the movie downstairs and your dad clanging around with pots, cleaning up in the kitchen. The aroma of lavender reminded me of something sad and sweet, a longing I couldn't quite place.

Then you looked at me.

For the first time you didn't look through me or away again but locked your gaze into mine with the dreamy determination of a sleepwalker balancing on a rooftop. I was instantly taken back to my first connection with Lele when we had danced around somebody's living room. With your eyes, you asked a simple but important question; I felt like I should know the answer. I didn't yet understand the question.

So, without thinking, I started talking to you.

I spoke in German, the language of our bedtime songs. I spoke of your first mother and how you must have missed her. I told you that I was strong enough for you to be sad and angry and even furious and wild. I told you it was safe to be whoever you are. I told you that I was your mother too and that you were my child; I told you that I would love you forever; all the while holding your gaze in mine. Slowly, like dewdrops gathering on a petal, your eyes filled and overflowed, silent teardrops spilling down your cheeks.

Time stood still.

Then you opened your mouth and the earth finally shook. You let out a primal scream of such anger, fear and despair that I shrank back for a heartbeat before I reached out again and gathered you against me.

You stiffened in my arms, stretching your limbs like wooden blocks against my body. Your feet kicked and your hands clawed at me and still you screamed.

I held you as close as I could while desperate sobs raced through your body like something wild had grabbed you by the neck and was shaking you and not letting go. I heard your dad run up the stairs. He stormed into the room and held out his arms to us, eyes wide, his face pale with fear.

I shook my head *no* at him. "It's OK," I said, my voice shaking with held back tears, "She needs to cry." He sat down on the floor with us.

You kicked and hit at me with renewed fury and I let go for fear of hurting you.

You ran out of the room, away from me, and threw yourself on the floor in the passage outside your bedroom. We followed you and sat down next to you. You carried on screaming and kicking, still in the grasp of the wild thing.

We just sat with you, big like mountains.

Tentatively I put a hand on your back and was relieved that you let me.

"It's OK, baby, cry. Cry as much as you need," was all I could say. Over and over I repeated these words. "It's OK, baby, you're safe now, cry as much as you need."

Slowly your sobs changed to a more regular rhythm, like the desperate cry of a small animal lost to her mother and hiding from predators in the dark.

I shivered as with a fever and for a moment I felt dizzy and closed my eyes. My face felt cold and wet. Your body shifted under my hand and when I opened my eyes again you were in your papa's arms, your sobs muffled against his chest.

I started to get up to check on your siblings, but as soon as I moved, you held out your hand and grabbed my arm, pulling me down again next to you and your dad. So I stayed and hugged you both.

You cried steadily for a while, a waterfall of tears spilling down your face.

After a long time you allowed me to get up and leave you with your papa. Downstairs in the lounge your siblings were still facing the TV, but the movie had come to an end and the title song was running on repeat over and over again. They sat like poppets frozen in time by the spell of an evil witch and I sat down between them, one arm around each familiar little body. They leaned in to me with what felt like a sigh. Lele was wiping her face on my arm. It was dark in the room but for the static spill of grey light from the TV. Outside the city lights sparkled and glittered. A breeze from the open window made the skin on my face tingle.

I kissed each head and reached for the remote in Kal's lap to press the pause button. The music stopped and for a while we silently listened to the sobs from upstairs and our own softer sniffles.

"Why is Nene so sad?" asked Kal, his voice shaky with tears.

"She misses Joanna, I think," I said.

"Did I also cry so much?" he asked me.

"It was different with you two," I said, "You were so much smaller, but, yes, you cried too."

"Is Joanna also sad?" Kal asked.

"I am sure she is, darling, I am sure she misses her, just as she missed you."

For a moment we all stared down the abyss that was the absence of Emily, Lele's first mother, in this conversation. She who never wanted to meet or even know about Lele was an absence that seemed to expand in my child's heart every time Joanna was mentioned.

I held Lele closer then. That was all I could do that night as sadness enveloped us like a thick mist coming off the mountain. "But why does she not keep her then?" Kal was quick to move on to his little sister again.

"Because she can't."

We were silent for a while, huddled into each other like climbers in a snowstorm cut off from the world below. "Sometimes," I said, "even though you make the right decision, you are still sad. Joanna wants Nene to have us as a family because she can't be all that Nene needs. But she will always be her mother – and yours – and she misses you both."

"Well, I don't miss her," said my clear and uncompromising child.

"That's OK, it has been a long time, and soon Nene won't miss her so much either and then someday, when you want to, we can maybe visit her."

"Never." Kal drew the line.

I felt Lele shift on my other side and held her tighter. She wouldn't ever speak of her sadness, but each night she climbed into my bed and crawled into my arms and maybe she found what she needed there. My fears like big black dogs were always biting at my heels whenever I thought about how bringing Kal's birth sister into our lives might make Lele even more withdrawn, emphasising a separateness she might have felt all her life.

"You can go back to her if you want, Mama," Kal said.

Lele nodded into my shoulder, "Yes, Mama, go, Papa can come and read us a story."

"Thank you," I said, "my big children. I love you."

I got up and climbed the stairs towards your inconsolable wailing. Without a word your papa put you in my arms, and you held onto me like you trusted me. I could hardly see your dad's face in the dark but I sensed that he too had been crying.

I picked up where I had left off.

"It's OK, baby, cry as much as you need. You are home now."

As the evening melted into night, your sobs turned into whimpers, interrupted only by an occasional hiccup and one last deep heart-sigh before you drifted into sleep.

When I put you in your cot that night, your sleeping face was clear like the sky after a thunderstorm and when you woke up the next morning, there was a new sparkle in your eyes, which has remained there ever since.

PART II

20

Black Wedding

May 2014, McGregor, South Africa

"And now, speaking for the bride, are our hosts, Alan and Martina. Please welcome them."

As I got up to make my way past smiling and clapping people towards the front of the gathering, I was thinking, not for the first time: *How did I get here?* and *I am so going to mess this up.*

Looking around me, barely breathing, I was also filled with a sense of pride, of a uniquely private achievement, like arriving in a foreign country after conquering a lifelong fear of flying. I noticed the two of you for once blending in with all the other kids lined up on the stairs behind the patio. Baby Nene, who had just joined our family a few weeks ago, was having her afternoon nap in the little room next to the kitchen. You were watching my every move and pretending not to, giggling and talking too loudly, masking your shyness behind outrageous statements and exaggerated gestures, "I can eat anything I want. I'll show you if you don't believe me, I can eat this flower," I heard one of you over the hushed conversations as soon as the clapping stopped.

I was waiting for your dad to make his way around our

table so we could walk up together and I saw Lele waving a rose from the wedding bouquet in an older girl's face. Most of the other kids were laughing, while some just looked, open-mouthed, at these two chatty strangers with their white parents. It seemed to be an honest, engaging curiosity, not a dismissive "othering" (*are you brown because your real mother didn't want you?*).

Eight-year-old Lele, all prettied up in white lace, glossy locks in a festive twist, attached herself to two beautiful teenagers in matching outfits, and Kal, sporting a mohawk with newly shorn sides, was parading up and down the stairs in a suit and a bow tie, charming the older girls with his cute boy routine. You both revelled in the attention, eyes and cheeks shining, high-pitched words tumbling out like jelly beans from a party pack.

The singing and ululating that went on throughout the home-cooked lunch had stopped and faces were peeping out from the kitchen door to listen to the speeches. There were 150 guests, seated on chairs wrapped in white fabric, at tables covered in more white fabric and dotted with pink and white rose petals. Most of the woven silver baskets for the fresh bread that we delivered last minute all the way from Cape Town were empty. People were sitting back, filling each other's champagne flutes, ready for the well-wishing and raising of glasses.

The men all wore dark suits, white shirts, and bow ties; the women out-glamoured the silver and white theme of the décor with an explosion of pinks and reds and oranges and violets and blues. Silky shawls with flowery designs, headdresses the size of a small house, and hats that looked like they had come with their own invitation were floating above the tables like an airborne audience of exotic birds.

Luckily, the day of the wedding came with sunny skies and the crisp freshness of washed linen fluttering in an early morning breeze. A few clouds dotted the horizon.

During the two-hour journey in the back of the car amidst a forest of ciabatta planks, the aroma of fresh baking made you hungry and whiney until your dad and I eventually saw reason and let you rip chunks out of a warm loaf, contradicting our previous warnings about sore tummies and you not being hungry for your lunch. That turned out to be a good decision. Lunch was delayed by several hours due to various late arrivals and a lengthier-than-anticipated ceremony, but mostly by the crowd of children, you among them, hovering near the bride-to-be like a swarm of bees excitedly buzzing around their queen, each one offering something sweet like a flower or a kiss or an urgent question:

"Can I have the top part of the wedding cake?"

"Are you going to have s. e. x. today?"

"What are you going to do with all the presents, can I help you unwrap?"

In the midst of the chaos, bags spilling shiny things, iPhones flashing and voices laughing, singing, whispering, and shouting, like a hidden treasure in a pass-the-parcel game, the bride stood, calm and casual in an over-washed, oversized flannel gown. She allowed you to pretend-help style her braids in an elegant up-do with tiny white flowers that looked like miniature daisies, as if this was just another day playing dress up with her favourite little people. You admired her silky dress, the colour of whipped cream, and watched in awe how it became alive, floating like a cloud around her body and stopping just so above her knees. You had never seen her in anything but sneakers or slippers, and could not get over the shiny shoes, in a colour called nude (clearly not with her skin-tone in mind) and with long spiky heels: "How are you not going to get stuck in the mud?"

Only if you knew her well could you sense nervousness from the twitch of a newly shaped eyebrow, the tremble in the corner of her mouth or the unfamiliar tinkle in her voice, the sound of delicate glass ornaments in a box of Christmas decorations rattled by an excited child. I wanted to hold her close, wrap her in layers of inspired assurances and offer a magic spell of eternal happiness, all the while aware that this was my own need to protect, my default instinct whenever I felt weakened by love. The bride did not need my magic spells; she just needed me to deliver a good speech.

Your dad and I wove our way towards the top table where the bride and groom were framed by a backdrop of white silk, suspended from the bamboo roof to hide the open braai behind it.

As I turned to face the wedding guests, my smile stretched a little too tight across my face. The aroma of roast chicken mixed with a medley of unfamiliar spices made me realise I hadn't eaten all day.

Before I knew it, Alan was freewheeling his part, confident and funny as usual. People laughed and clapped. Looking down at my hands tightly gripping the gold-coloured folder with my ten-minute speech printed out in oversized letters (just in case I forgot my glasses), I noticed sweaty fingerprints all over the cover. An adult turned to hush the kids, still chatting and giggling on the stairs.

Alan was coming to the end of his impromptu introduction and too soon it would be my turn. As I put on my glasses, I felt heat creeping up from my neck, covering my cheeks.

My whole life I had managed to avoid public speaking, shuddering at the idea like I would at the thought of a dreaded disease. My fears of being reduced to a stuttering and blushing cartoon version of myself the moment more than two pairs of eyes were trained on me kept me away from any group events involving talking sticks and let's-go-round-the-circle-type introductions. Even though I have connected the dots back to my wounded child, wept on my therapist's shoulder, and learned the necessary affirmations, it still took a lot out of me to raise my hand and say my bit at your kindergarden parent-teacher meetings.

I am only telling you this so you understand: this was a really big deal for me. The fact that I was one of the few white faces among all these people who were mostly strangers to me did nothing to calm my nerves.

So how did I wrestle my public speaking panic to the ground for this woman whom I hadn't even known two years before, and who had asked me, her white friend, not only to host her wedding but stand up and talk for her on this day?

As I was standing beside her on her wedding day, with burning cheeks and a nervous twitch to my mouth, her eyes were holding me with a calm confidence that I didn't think I deserved. I only hoped I wouldn't have to see myself on somebody's phone or laptop later. If I could have, I would have disappeared in a puff of smoke. I opened my gold-coloured folder, adjusted my glasses, and read my first ever speech, for my children, my colourful hopes, and my beautiful friend on her wedding day.

21

A Person My Colour

I had met Tumi two years earlier. She was slouching in the corner of my grey-green living room couch, the fading light coming in through the big windows behind her and casting her features in gloomy shadows. She had the body and posture of a defiant teenage boy, one stockinged foot on the coffee table, eyes luminous under her cropped afro, extending an unspoken challenge to the world in general and to me in particular: *who are you, white woman, with your black kids and a fucking palace in suburbia, serving designer soup and heat-to-eat ciabatta fresh from the oven, all the while hosting a privileged group of women to talk about r a c e of all things?* Her eyes seemed to be looking right through me.

I eyed her back warily, her obstinate presence raising my eyebrows and my defences: after all, she was in my house and who was she to judge me? Anyway, I had black kids, so I knew what it was like, and that made me one of the good people, right?

She also made it clear from the start that she hadn't joined our group to make friends. She was here to monitor what we were up to and inject some reason into the conversation when it would turn all "kumbaya" (race doesn't matter, we are all just humans who can overcome our differences and love each other). I had joined the group recently on the invitation of one of your friend's mums, Jan. I knew from snippets of conversations we had around school drop-offs and pick-ups that Jan questioned her role as a white South African and had gathered a few women from "diverse" backgrounds some months earlier to start conversations about race. When she called me one afternoon to ask if I wanted to stand in for someone white who had cancelled short notice, I dropped the spoon in the soup on the stove, left Alan in charge, and came running. Despite my fear of anything cliquey (I had so far successfully dodged book clubs, adoption groups, and mums-and-tots gatherings), this was one group I really wanted to join.

Ever since my botched promenade conversation with B, I knew I needed to do more than just read a few books or have some inconsequential Facebook conversations with adult adoptees from the U.S. in order to catch up with my changed reality. I knew it was vital for me to face whatever "it" was and that I would not find all the answers online or in books: I needed to talk to and connect with black people. Not the black people whom I paid, or who worked for the white people I knew, but black people who would not be afraid to tell me the truth. About what, I was as yet unclear. I knew I was in no position to meet the questions you were starting to ask, and I could no longer ignore the observations you made about a world in which white people were in charge and black people in service.

"Papa, can a person my colour ever drive a fancy car like that?" Lele had asked one day. She was three years old, pointing a chubby finger at a Porsche or BMW, nose pressed to the window of Alan's Ford bakkie as he was taking her on one of their Sunday cruises through a car wash. He came home that afternoon deeply shaken and unsure of what to do. His, "Of course you can. You can do anything you want my darling," was glaringly inadequate in the face of her reality, like covering a heap of dog shit on our well-tended lawn in pink paint and calling it a flower. I realised then that you would never believe what we told you. We had nothing to show for our version of the world. Telling you how we loved your brown skin and people who looked like you (*of course brown people can have important jobs too, darling*), all the while socialising in exclusively white circles, where black people cleaned up after our parties, was damaging to your growing minds.

I felt like an abuser telling my victim that the abuse was a sign of my love, all the while fearing that one day you would see the truth and hate me. I was scared. I was ashamed. I was overwhelmed by an ever-growing sadness, a landslide of rock-hard truths piling up on top of me.

Changing my life bit by bit was not really a choice. I would have to either close my eyes and continue pretending, or begin to scramble my way out of this heap of white lies. To start somewhere, I decided I might as well try and talk to black people, hoping like hell they would want to talk to me. So when Jan told me about the group, I wanted to be there more than I had ever wanted to be anywhere.

This was my second meeting, and I had offered our newly renovated home. Between greeting arrivals and serving food, I went upstairs to put you to bed, which back then still involved a song each and always a whispered conversation under your duvets. You were giggly and wide awake and curious; so many new people in our house, so many people who looked like you.

"What are you going to talk about, Mama?"

"Mama, who is the beautiful lady with the long braids?"

"Where does she live?"

"Is she from South Africa?"

"Who is the lady with all the bangles, did she come in that fancy car?"

"Do you know her?"

"What is Jan doing here? Did she bring Jack and Lilly?"

"Shhh, sleep now, I'll tell you all in the morning." I kissed sweet smelling cheeks, tugged duvets around warm bodies and fluffy toys, glad for these few moments of soothing routine to contain my nervous excitement.

When I rejoined the group in my living room, more people had arrived, one of them Tumi, briefly sizing me up with her unforgiving stare.

The conversation was already in full swing. An agitated Thandeka was busy recounting her shopping experiences at the local drug store, where she would inevitably be followed through the aisles by a security guard. Her nose was twitching as she was telling us how she challenged the guard who would not admit that he had targeted her by orders of his superiors. Her delicate features, perfectly arched eyebrows over fiercely intelligent eyes, and the smallest ears peeping out between her shoulder-long braids, seemed to be at odds with a voice that commanded attention and a body firmly grounded like a meditating Buddha. Thandeka took groups to the mountains for a living with themes like "Death and Dying" or "Telling our Stories". She looked fashionable without being flashy, in jeans and boots and a leather jacket. She was not followed by store detectives because she looked destitute and in need of stealing hygiene products, if that even qualifies as an identifiable look. She was followed because she was black.

"That must be so painful," Di commented, "to be assumed a criminal just because of the colour of your skin."

Di, Jan's friend from school and married to a black man with two biracial children, had wrapped herself in one of my woolly blankets, her highlighted bob swinging from side to side as she shook her head in angry sympathy.

"It's called racial profiling and it's everywhere," Tumi clarified, ice in her voice.

"But are you sure the security guard is not following everybody, also the white people?" A woman with short reddish hair, pale cheeks slightly flushed, big grey eyes behind frameless glasses, sincerely inquisitive, was on the path of truth-finding.

I was still holding back, afraid to say the wrong things and be seen as a racist. I would not have dared to ask, but the question made sense to me. I saw lots of security guards in many of the stores I shopped in. Since I never paid much attention to anybody, I hadn't noticed if they followed me. Frankly, I didn't think I'd care.

"Have you ever been followed?" Tumi asked back, head raised like a cobra in striking mode.

"Um, I don't know," the woman said, a note of defiance creeping into her voice, "When I walk around Woodstock Main Road, I also get profiled as the fat white lady whom men can take advantage of and sell stuff to at double price."

"So you're saying being black is like being fat?" Tumi faultlessly delivered the strike.

"No!" Her denial was coming out close to a shout. "What I am saying is that it's not just black people who are targeted. As a single overweight woman, I know what it's like." She pushed her reddish fringe back from her forehead, tugged at her ponytail, and crossed her legs and arms, eyes flickering around the room in search of sympathy.

I watched the exchange with a mixture of fascination, horror and great relief that I wasn't the one in the hot seat. I wasn't sure who irritated me more, the whiney white woman or the aggressive black activist.

After an uncomfortable silence, Jan, my tall naturally blonde mum-friend with the prettiness of an American cheerleader, managed to bring us all back to the safety of firm politeness with her air of calm detachment. "I think the point here is, Mag, that we are talking about the experience of black women in a racist society. What you are referring to might be another conversation for another group, but for now we should stick with our mandate, which is to explore race in post-Apartheid South Africa and how it affects us all differently."

All-round relieved nods and tentative smiles. Mag slunk back into her seat, lips pursed in a five-year-old's sulk, and grabbing one of my red and grey couch pillows like she was going to throttle the life out of it. Tumi resumed her slouch, pointedly looking out the window, or maybe just contemplating the view of the city lights that had come on in the meantime, sparkling like a thousand Christmas trees in the distance below us. The evening carried on with civilised talk around prejudice and privilege, and I mentally took notes of terms like "white privilege", "eurocentricism", "structural racism" and others I was going to Google the next day.

When we said our goodbyes, Tumi avoided the round of hugs and I did not expect to see her back the next time. But she surprised me. I never saw Mag again.

There was this one evening, maybe a year or so into our meetings, when the person who was supposed to facilitate the session and introduce a new subject for the group to discuss hadn't shown up. We were all sitting around waiting, getting a little drunk on red wine and a new cozy familiarity. Somebody suggested this would be a good time to come out with our worst learned prejudices. At first nobody bit. We all looked at each other, reluctant to embarrass ourselves.

Thandeka started tentatively, "White people love their dogs more than they care about black people." We white people looked at each other, not sure whether to defend or attack, but then somebody let out a stifled giggle.

Jan took a deep breath and offered bravely, "Black people are always late."

Followed by more giggles and a prompt retort, "White people can't dance."

"Black people are bad drivers," was immediately countered with, "White people make an ostrich face whenever they greet black people." By now we were all shouting above one another, stereotypes flying across the room on near-hysterical laughter. When we ran out of prejudices, we asked each other questions we had all wondered about at some point but never asked anybody.

"What is it with that hand-cream all black girls carry around in their handbags?" and "Why do white people always expect you to bring food when they invite you?" or a little more daring, "Is that real hair on your head?"

Eventually we ventured into multi-cultural sex talk:

"What do white girls like in bed?"

"Do black girls shave or wax their privates?"

"Do you have a Hollywood or a landing strip?"

"OMG, I can't believe you just asked me that," Thando shrieked, head thrown back, one gold looped earring getting caught up in a braid.

"Do you guys watch porn, what kind of?" came from Tumi, who looked about 15 years old, eyes bright with mischief.

"How often do you have sex with your boyfriends/husbands?" The questions kept coming, peppered here and there with single word answers followed by more raucous laughter.

Later still, we were talking *Sex in the City* style, huddled together on the carpet amongst pillows and blankets, arms draped around shoulders, hands casually resting on somebody else's leg, heads close together, an easy intimacy enveloping us like a blanket on a cold night. For a few hours we nearly forgot what was supposed to divide us; instead our differences became the focus of uncensored curiosity and liberating laughter. At the end of the evening, high on girl talk, our hugs warm and firm, we felt like best friends... until the next meeting when reality set in once again and showed us our fragile boundaries.

22

Meeting Your Mama

Let me interrupt your mama here for a moment. She just told you how she and I got to know each other and, as I am in the story now, I thought I'd tell you what it was like for me, meeting you for the first time.

At the time I joined the dialogue group I was unemployed. I was invited by my friend Thandeka, who was recruited by a white senior manager from her work with whom she felt uncomfortable in a social setting. I mainly went to support her, but also felt it might be an interesting group to check out. White people from the group were not normally people I had access to in my daily life and I was intrigued by the idea that they wanted to talk about race and racism with us.

It was a couple of sessions after we had started. We were told we would be having another white member join the group. I didn't remember us discussing this new membership as a collective but someone (read: white person) decided to do so. To my surprise, we were having our session at the new member's house. I entered her house feeling a bit angry because of how things happened. I had been part of the group from the first session and we had not even discussed going to my house for a session and yet here we were, sitting at this white woman's fancy triple-storey house in the mountains. I don't think I had ever been in a house this big before.

I sat in the corner towards the end of the room to allow myself not to participate if I didn't feel like it. I missed the beginning of the dialogue; I was too busy scanning the room and wondering what it must feel like to live in such a place. I also felt a little annoyed by her. She didn't act like a new member at all; one would swear she had always been there. Something about the way she carried herself upset me. She acted like she belonged to the group though she had only been part of it for five minutes ... and oh man did she have a big nose. I in hindsight realise that she did belong, more so than I, because the group was in actual fact a white group. We, the blacks, were ornamental.

We went around the room introducing ourselves. I remember feeling intimidated by the introductions where people talked about what they do: we had managers, business owners, lecturers etc. I have grown to hate doing this. I think there are more creative ways of introducing ourselves without creating hierarchies. I remember your mama talking about how she had started studying again. I found this particularly annoying. I had just gone through the frustrating process of getting a loan for my studies and here was this white woman studying because she has the money, to pass time. The dialogue moved on and to this day I do not remember what we spoke about. At some point I faded out of the conversation and was captured by the bright city lights shining from the window. I stared out for a while appreciating the view, the mountain and the clear skies. I tried to spot places or buildings that I knew. My gaze went further and further trying to locate my house in Gugulethu, on the other side of town. But it might as well have been on a different planet, my reality felt so far removed from this place and the people I was with.

I heard voices from the stairs and figured our new dialogue member had kids.

Then you, Lele and Kal walked in giggling and blushing (Nene wasn't born yet). My first reaction was surprise that you were not white and then I figured your mama must be married to a black man. As I watched you interact with her, I found myself smiling. The love between you guys was so vibrant. I noticed how your mama's appearance changed when she was interacting with the two of you. She seemed like a totally different person. She had looked cold, arrogant, distant, and a know-it-all just a minute ago, but then turned into someone warm and loving when you two shoved your bodies into hers trying to hide from all the strangers in your house.

Your papa came down to fetch you and I was all kinds of confused when I saw a tall, bald white man. You put up quite a fight but eventually gave in. Your papa carried both of you off to bed. Your mama continued giggling after you left, cracked a joke or two, and then drifted back to her initial look of arrogance.

23

Awkward Birthday Party

Our dialogue group was still in its infancy and none of us were quite ready yet to venture beyond the limitations of polite and cautious. One day, when Tumi's transport hadn't worked out and she was stranded in town I offered her a bed and a lift to work the next day.

It didn't occur to me at the time that some of the black people in the group routinely took it upon themselves to travel far distances on public transport or had to beg lifts from people, who in turn waited for them or went out of their way to pick their friends up. Did I assume the benefits of talking about racism to white women outweighed the inconveniences involved? Sure, I knew about poor people and the glaring inequalities in our society, but mine was a knowledge that mainly came from clichés (*eat your soup child, the poor kids in Africa are starving*) overused by German parents to teach their children lessons of an abstract moral value, not something directly connected to people I knew.

Tumi stayed over for the first time that day and we ended up talking through the night. Her intolerance of everything superficial and her barely disguised vulnerability behind a tough no-nonsense act was like an eerily familiar side of me that I had always felt ashamed of and could now admire in somebody else.

As time went by we found fragile tendrils of connection beyond our skin tones. After our tense and loaded dialogue evenings, we often huddled together on the sofa under duvets, feeling a closeness that surprised us both as we sat long into the night unwrapping parts of our stories, like carefully selected gifts for one another.

I tended to our budding friendship with invitations, texts, and phone calls, finding myself in the exposed and forceful role of the pursuer, a role I had avoided my whole life. To my surprise I learned in the process that friendship, like a wish whispered with the determination of a child, can be a gift of one's own making.

Apart from our late night conversations on my couch, there seemed to be no spaces for our worlds to meet, where an "us" could grow and develop. For the longest time, our friendship did not feel "normal". When we were out together shopping or at a restaurant, people visibly noticed us with a double take, trying to work us out. The assumption was that Tumi was working for me or we were lovers. Black people asked her in isiXhosa about her "Madam" and why I would make her work on a weekend. White people would give us a look of exaggerated approval, or a tightly stretched smile, even a few winks. Some looked confused or angry.

I tried to join my two increasingly separate worlds. I even overcame my fear of hosting parties and planned a birthday party so that I could introduce my new dialogue friends to my old, mainly white, friends.

I invited almost everybody I knew: women from a book-club I had joined years back but hardly ever participated in, some from my weekly dance group, some mums of your school friends and of course everybody from our dialogue group. It was going to be a Saturday afternoon garden party. In true Cape Town style, everybody accepted the invitation, but that didn't mean people would actually show up.

On the morning of the party I was jittery with nerves. What if nobody came? Who would be the first to arrive?

Would I have to make awkward conversation with someone I barely knew? Would people connect or stay separate in their own circles? What would I do if somebody said something racist? What if the whole afternoon would just be one long uncomfortable silence? What had I done? Was it too late to pretend I was sick and call the whole thing off?

Alan as usual calmed me down and promised it would all be just wonderful.

It wasn't. It also was.

Thandeka was the first to arrive. She had travelled by minibus-taxi from Gugulethu and the driver had dropped her at a corner a few streets away from our house. As she wasn't familiar with the neighbourhood she had stopped at somebody's house and asked for directions.

"Sjoe," she puffed as she made her way up the stairs to our front door, looking stylish as usual, in black boots, jeans, leather jacket and oversized handbag. "I nearly got arrested loitering around your neighbourhood."

"Oh no, what happened?" I was mortified.

"Agh, just the usual," she flicked her braids over her shoulder and shrugged her jacket off. I took the jacket and her bag from her and dropped both on the couch opposite our front door.

"When I asked for directions, this person gave me one scared look and ran back into their house. Then she observed me through the window while talking into her cellphone, probably calling Neighbourhood Watch," she continued.

"Are you OK?" I asked.

"I am fine," she sighed, following me into the kitchen, where I had set up drinks and snacks on the counter. She poured herself a glass of orange juice.

"Do you want some champagne with that?" I held the bottle out to her.

"Yes please," she grinned. "Pass the bottle why don't you."

I smiled back, unsure about what to say or ask or whether I should just drop the issue. She drank half her glass of orange juice in one go and topped up with champagne. For a while we didn't speak. She checked her phone. I re-arranged some platters.

"So how did you find your way in the end?" I eventually asked.

"Being the good black of course," she shrugged as if this was stating the obvious.

I didn't dare ask.

"I just told the next person I saw in their front yard that I was applying for a job as a cleaner and was lost and late, and worried I might not get the job. So the woman took pity on the black girl, got her car keys out and dropped me outside your door."

I joined in with her laughter, a little too loud.

Raising her glass as if about to make a toast, she walked across the room and looked out the window towards the driveway.

"Oh good she's left – I am not sure how I would explain to her that I am sipping champagne in your lounge. Remind me to drive my car to your house next time."

She waved out the window, where Tumi was busy parking her scooter next to the neighbour's gold BMW. I buzzed the gate open. As soon as she entered the house (hey, happy birthday are we the first ones?) Thandeka launched into her story of how she had been chauffeured to my front door by a benevolent white neighbour. Tumi rolled her eyes, emptied Thandeka's glass and they both made their way to the kitchen, laughing and shaking their heads. I stared open mouthed at Tumi's bright red t-shirt imprinted with the silhouette of a woman's afro over big black letters spelling DARKIE.

I put her stuff down and followed them into the kitchen to pour myself a glass of champagne. I usually don't drink.

That first glass of champagne on an empty stomach soon inserted a layer of insulation between me and my surroundings. I felt comfortably detached, while remaining aware of everything that was happening around me, or so I thought. I can't quite remember where you or your dad were in all of this.

What I do remember are the awkward moments like random snapshots laid out without order or context.

My white friends came trickling in soon after Tumi and Thandeka's arrival. First a few mothers from your school, followed by a group from my dancing class in floating garments, and lastly some book-club friends. Somebody had brought a guitar and they played happy birthday for me outside on the patio, which made me blush and cringe. Soon all my white friends surrounded the guitar for more singalongs outside on the patio, while a small group of black women gathered around the kitchen counter, hooting with laughter at what I supposed was Thandeka's account of her white-suburbia-experience. I was on my second glass by then and stood a little bemused between the two groups, one foot on the patio, one foot in the kitchen.

Tumi showed a picture on her cellphone to the group at the counter. Raucous laughter followed. One of my mum friends left the singing and strumming on the patio to get a plate of food and was swept up in the hilarity caused by Tumi's phone. She asked to see the picture and I followed her in, looking over her shoulder as Tumi angled it towards us. The picture on the screen was a meme I had previously seen on Facebook: a white man's face, cheeks unnaturally stretched into a grimace of forced friendliness and the caption, "the face white people make when greeting a black person in their neighbourhood."

"It's called the ostrich face," Tumi explained helpfully, between giggles.

The group snorted with renewed laughter and I heard

myself join in. The white mum turned red and glared at me. My laugh caught in my throat and I tried to mask it with a hasty sip of champagne that turned into a cough.

"They are so racist," she hissed in my ear, hitting me between the shoulder blades, "Why are you putting up with this?"

"It's just a bit of fun," I apologised. "Don't take it personally."

"And what's with the t-shirt?" She was pointing at Tumi's back, eyes narrowed. "How is this even OK?" We had stepped away from the kitchen counter, me coughing, her slapping my back, and she continued, allowing her anger to take over.

"We are not even allowed to describe a person as black anymore, which is ridiculous when you think how the newspapers can't even describe them when a black person commits a crime – so how is it OK for her to wear this t-shirt and at your party. If they don't like white people and only want to provoke us, why are they even here?"

I thought she might be a little drunk and tried to get her away from the kitchen counter, but I needn't have worried. Nobody paid any attention to her ramblings; they were much too absorbed in their own conversation.

All I could think about was the imminent disaster I needed to avoid, the fighting that might follow if somebody heard her and took her on, dialogue style. So I shushed her and steered her towards a couch in the lounge, where I deposited her with a plate of food and a full glass of champagne, her blonde head barely peeping across the rust coloured backrest.

Then Jackie, a bookclub member I barely knew, crossed from the patio to the kitchen counter and found herself filling her plate next to a guest who didn't quite match the profile of white suburban Cape Town. Uncomfortable introductions were made, "Hi, I am Jackie," the "hi" stretching over several vowels, hand extended, "I don't believe we have met."

"Hi, Jackie, my name is Vuyelwa, nice to meet you." Matter-of-fact voice, shaking of hands.

"Sorry, I didn't get that. Was it Vuya?"

"Vu-ye-l-wa." Slowly this time.

"Oh OK, Vuyla," with a little laugh, "I'll probably ask you again in a minute, I am so bad with names and faces, but it's really nice to meet you."

"Sure, no problem Jackie," Vuyelwa said with a smile before turning back to the conversation that had been interrupted by the introduction.

After everybody had eaten and an army of empty bottles filled up the sink, people started mingling more freely. I remember my white friends ascending on the group of black women with an air of welcoming benevolence, as if to prove they were not scared of them (*So, how do you and Martina know each other? Where did you go to school, you speak so well?*). Some ventured into political territory, maybe genuinely interested in a "black point of view" (*So, what do you guys think about your government? My cleaning lady says black men are lazy – is she racist?*).

I hovered on the sidelines, trying to convey to my black friends that I got it, I wasn't white like that – anymore – a measured eye roll at somebody's back my only argument. At the same time I wanted to save my white friends from being exposed as racists and/or leaving with their feelings hurt and hating me for it. Adding to my confusion was the fact that I recognised myself in all of them. Before the dialogue group started opening my eyes to the many casual transgressions we as white people commit or simply overlook, I would have made an ass of myself with my unintentional racist questions and ignorant comments. That I had learned to shut up when in doubt wasn't something to feel proud or superior about.

By late afternoon most of my white friends had left. A small group of dialogue people and a few late comers remained, sitting around the big patio table. The atmosphere suddenly seemed more relaxed (or maybe it was me) and I found myself enjoying myself for the first time that day.

One white person chirped, "This is so awesome, I feel like I have gone to sleep and woken up at a UN convention," and everybody laughed together.

Somebody else explained our dialogue concept in reply to a question about how we all knew each other, and people listened with genuine interest. A handful of us remained sitting and talking until long after dark.

Tumi and Thandeka slept in the guest room that night and we spent the next day together, eating leftovers outside on the daybed and taking turns entertaining you. When Tumi took you to the park for a few hours you came back bright eyed and glowing with laughter. She told us how you had interrogated her the entire time about boyfriends and relationships and when she had said she wasn't quite sure if and when she would like to marry her (now husband) boyfriend, four year old Kal had told her, serious and concerned, "You should know Tumi, because communication is very important in a relationship."

Soon after that weekend, my white mum-friend called me to say she didn't want to be friends anymore.

"You have changed," she said accusingly and when I didn't make much effort to disagree, she drove her point home more forcefully, "So and so also think so, we don't understand what you are doing sucking up to all these people with whom you have nothing in common. They are racist and not your friends and if you can't see this, there is something seriously wrong with you."

That was the last time I tried to mix my two worlds. Partly by choice but mainly because I had hardly any white friends left, I focused even more on making black friends.

For the longest time that meant hovering awkwardly around black people whenever and wherever I met them. I felt a bit like a stalker, trying to get a phone number, a playdate, or raise some interest in our dialogue group. Many people didn't know what to make of me and my labouring attempts at closeness. To them it was just weird, a white woman trying to make friends.

I got brushed off a lot.

I also felt hurt by the "guilty by association" stamp that did not acknowledge my individual "goodness" in this new (to me) hostile, racialised terrain. I felt as if I had stumbled into a parallel universe where my feelings were not the most important, my pain not the sole focus, and my opinions not the most crucial in the room.

I lived with a constant feeling of unease, like I had just found out I was born with a faulty gene. There were many moments when I longed for the ignorance and oblivion of my previous life and when I fantasised about taking the next flight out of this mess so I could hide in familiar landscapes, amongst *my people*, where skin tone would not determine who I was; where I could feel safe and accepted for simply being me.

Only to realise that you were now *my people* and you would never have that choice.

As your mother, neither did I.

For the first time in my life I got a sense of what it might feel like to be judged because of the colour of my skin.

24

Are You a Rice-ist?

Let me tell you about our first dinner party with a selection of random strangers we had met at different social events and who – to my surprise – had all agreed to come; about my nervousness, the claustrophobic feeling of being in the spotlight, playing to an audience whose language I didn't speak; about your big eyes as you realised that for the first time in your lives your mama and papa were the only white people in the room.

Alan was making a fire in the lounge, Sade singing softly in the background, and the two of you (Nene was not born yet) had your noses pressed against the big window in our entrance hall waiting for our guests to appear. I had styled Lele's locks all morning, an art that I was slowly learning with the help of YouTube and an unending supply of DVDs; Kal, thankfully, still preferred mohawks.

"They're here, they're here!" and, "Wow, look at the car, Papa, that's a BMW!" you shrieked as you jumped up and down with excitement before the first two guests had even climbed out of their car.

Alan had met Max, a journalist from Zimbabwe, in a bar on Long Street a few weeks previously. They spent hours talking and drinking together and at the end of the evening exchanged numbers and promises to meet up again. When Alan invited him, he accepted without hesitation, saying he would bring someone. From Alan's description of Max (tall, handsome, glamorous), I expected him to arrive with an equally stylish woman, maybe an artist or a model.

Max was indeed tall and handsome with polished city-looks, black designer jeans, frameless spectacles, a shaved head, and several gold rings on his dancing hands. His smile was bright and reassuring with a professional edge to it like a doctor explaining a serious but not hopeless condition to his patient. His partner Sbu, on the other hand, looked like a black Che Guevara, including red beret, facial hair, and fierce eyes scanning his surroundings in a way that made me feel hopelessly white and middle-class. He was also wearing jeans that were ripped at both knees and a black hoodie. When he shook my hand, he looked right through me, igniting a trembling panic in my bones.

What the hell had I been thinking inviting total strangers into our home, hoping that ... what? They would applaud my newfound sense of diversity and obligingly play the role of token black friends in my life? That they would break out in happy smiles the moment they set eyes on my children and congratulate me on my rainbow family?

Thinking of which, where were my children? There were giggles coming from the top of the stairs, and I quickly called you to the rescue, "Come say hello to our guests!" You giggled some more and didn't budge.

Luckily before the moment turned into irreversible awkwardness, I saw Thuli and Bongile standing outside our gate, a couple we had met at a party a few weeks back. The hosts also had an adopted daughter who was going to playgroup with Lele, and I had sat with the mum through some playdates and birthday parties. The invitation to her husband's birthday celebration came a bit out of the blue, but Alan and I decided to make an effort (meeting other adoptive parents was strongly advised by all).

In the end, we nearly didn't make it, struggling to get out of the house between tears and promises (to be back before you woke up, to bring you some birthday cake, to tell the babysitter you could watch movies until you passed out, to buy you Ferraris on your eighteenth birthdays). When we eventually arrived at the crowded restaurant somewhere in the suburbs, everybody was already seated at a long table, a cabaret show in full swing on an elevated stage the size of a cheap hotel bathroom.

I noticed her the moment we arrived, maybe because of the strapless red velvet dress setting her skin aglow or her self-contained, somewhat queenly smile which seemed to reflect an inner state of being rather than a fleeting expression of politeness or affection.

Without asking (everybody was too busy clapping and singing along to some '70s number), I took a chair from a neighbouring table and squeezed in next to her. After the song ended, I introduced myself and we spent the evening talking on and off about anything from clothes to food to hair and the daily challenges of educating black kids in white schools. Her eyes were a little slanted and heavy lidded, giving the impression of somebody half-asleep and playfully alert at the same time, like a Siamese cat contemplating a chirping bird from her velvety window seat. I felt over-eager and out of my depth, like auditioning for a part I hadn't rehearsed properly.

Her husband Bongile reminded me of a character in an animated movie, all giggles and soft unfocused eyes behind gold-framed spectacles and a voice like honey. There was also a steely edge to him, an aura like an invisible cloak that could turn him from friendly bear to monster-slaying super hero in the blink of an eye. Alan quickly bonded with him over wine menus and manly jokes, and at the end of the evening we had their phone numbers and a promise they would come to dinner.

When they rang our doorbell, I was so relieved that I made a bit of a show waving and smiling enthusiastically through the window (*see, Sbu? I am not the typical White Woman you think I am, I have other black friends to prove it …*). The squeals of delight that erupted the moment they entered our house had me step back in confusion (maybe it was a black thing?) as they both sailed right past me to exchange hugs and high-fives with Max and Sbu. It turned out they knew each other from long-ago Johannesburg times.

We all discussed this coincidence for a while, and then the four of them settled into an easy chatter, leaving me to contemplate the long evening ahead, the familiar feeling of being out of place, and wishing I were elsewhere. So I kept myself busy with clanging pots (I had made two different dishes, rice and pasta, just in case) and installing you two with bowls of pasta at the little kiddies' table in front of the fire, where you sat and stared, forkfuls of food suspended halfway to your mouths, eyes darting between the four strangers like you had front row seats to "Disney on Ice".

The last to arrive were Kate and Mkhombandlela. I had met her (New York English literature professor from Trinidad, mother to a two-year-old, and married to a South African) at a dialogue social a few weeks back and could not stop staring at her. She had the calm confidence of someone used to speaking to an attentive audience and a slow, deliberate way of stringing words into artful and intricate sentences, drawing her listeners in. She also had the fashion sense of a *Vogue* cover model, a mix of classic elegance and daring innovation: vintage dress accessorised with edgy boots and chunky pieces of jewellery shining on her skin like strange, colourful stars; natural hair styled in a glamorous up-do, defying the South African beauty myth of relaxed hair, weaves, and extensions; and eyes the soft glow of mahogany dipped in honey.

I was too intimidated to ask for her number that evening, but when I bumped into her a few weeks later, both of us trudging around a mall with tired kids and trolleys full of groceries, her spontaneous greeting (*Hey, Martina, right?*) across the aisle emboldened me to invite her to my dinner party later that week.

Her husband Mkhombandlela (I had spent the day practising his name at traffic lights, while cooking dinner and in front of the bathroom mirror) looked the picture of distracted professor (blue shirt under red woollen sweater with leather elbow patches, ironed jeans, and mustard suede college shoes including the tassels) who had been dragged out of the house in the midst of putting together an important piece of research. He had a friendly distant smile and didn't say much. Clearly socialising was not his thing.

The others got on with talking and reminiscing (Kate and Thuli happened to be best friends.) From my vantage point at the kitchen island overlooking the dining table, I could not shake the feeling that I had gate-crashed my own party, a big pale moon trying to fit in with the stars.

When it was time to serve the food, everybody politely stopped talking and helped pass things around the table. Sbu took one look at the bowl I held out to him and said, "No, thanks, I hate rice."

"Luckily, I made some pasta," I heard the strain in my cheer as I put the bowl down and reached for the pasta dish. Before I could stop myself, I added, "Are you a rice-ist then?"

The joke hovered in the air like an unpleasant smell. My armpits started itching and my face felt like it had turned the puce colour of the pasta sauce. The music had stopped some time ago and the only sounds in the room were the soft brush of rain against glass and the scrabble of my serving spoon.

Then a giggle came from Bongile, eyes glinting with mischief as something passed between him and Sbu, and they both burst out laughing, heads shaking, hands clapping shoulders, sweeping the other along in a wave of mirth.

"That was the worst joke ever," Bongile puffed, wiping tears from his eyes.

I threw the spoon in the bowl, fell back on my chair, and laughed with them.

"White people's jokes," Sbu agreed, but he winked at me as he fished the spoon out of the sauce and loaded up his plate.

"It's like when they tell you don't worry, the dog is fine, just don't show it you're scared." Bongile was still laughing.

"Or, 'Can I help you?' when you're parking your car in a white neighbourhood," Thuli chirped in.

"Yo, I was worried your neighbours would call Armed Response when we were standing outside your gate earlier." Bongile turned to Alan, boxing him on the shoulder.

"They probably have," said Alan, my rock, my best friend, love of my life, and best papa in the world as he sat there smiling and relaxed, like he had just popped in to watch a game with his mates.

And just like that I found myself on the other side, still me, still white, still not "one of them", yet somehow included. I felt like I was a child again, walking home from school in early winter darkness, past brightly lit windows where strangers lived out my fantasies of family and belonging, and all of a sudden finding myself on the inside, amongst a family of welcoming strangers, disoriented and comforted at the same time.

Here was an insight into yet another facet of the parallel universe I had discovered a while ago. From where I had raged and fought with the zeal of a guilty bystander, isolated by my new status (mother of black children) and new-found awareness, yet forever fused to the perpetrators, there was no space for light-heartedness. On the other side of the racial divide, however, righteous anger comes with a price. Sometimes laughter is the only way to carry on.

After the mirthful prelude, we sat and talked until long after midnight (you passed out on the couch sometime during the second or third movie), like we had collectively opened up a vent into a previously airless room and couldn't stop the swirls and streams of words, following the threads of our differing experiences to places none of us had ever ventured in the company of the other.

My father got his degree in England because he was not allowed to operate on white people here; the first time I ever saw white people working on the side of the road, or riding on the back of a garbage truck, was in Europe; wherever I go, as soon as there are white people, I am always conscious of my blackness; I hate white people; the worst thing about racism is that it robs me of the ability to accept criticism.

I was brought up fearing the black man who came in the company of Santa Claus, punishing naughty children; I remember this song, "Ten Little Negroes", which taught us to count backwards (and then there was only one).

Before I came to South Africa, I was a woman first; now I am first black and then a woman.

Before I had my children, I just was a good person; now I am always guilty because I am white; I never knew I was racist until I became a mother to black children.

Long after everyone had left, Alan and I sat in front of the dying fire, soaking up the last bit of warmth, reliving parts of the evening, not wanting it to end, as if we were afraid the next day would break the spell and we would be cast back into our respective corners, strangers once again.

25

The Shopping Trip

When I saw Tumi's name on the display of my phone, I took my lunch to my room and settled down for a few minutes of catch-up, which had become our routine every few days. It was a Saturday, your dad had taken you out for the afternoon and I had a few blissful hours to myself.

When I answered her call, hoping we would finalise a plan to get together, she didn't say much. I jumped in with some chatter about my week, still unsure about our silences and how much I was allowed to dig or disclose. Whenever we ventured beyond the space of our dialogue group issues, my children (you loved her with the ear-piercing, all-consuming intensity only four- and six-year-olds are capable of), and shared or individual experiences of day-to-day racism, I was always hyperaware of my whiteness and how it infiltrated almost every aspect of our friend-ship. Was I using her to make myself less toxic to you as a mother? Would she always see my whiteness first? Was it possible, necessary, or maybe futile to try and separate skin colour from our friendship?

Whenever I voiced my confusion and doubts, she laughed at me and said, "Congratulations, you are just having a black experience."

My glass bubble had cracked. Knowing seeped in every day. Here we were again.

Her silence made me chatter on until I ran out of safe

stuff to say. I waited for her to say something.

"I am going to sell my bike," she eventually told me.

"Why now, you're using it all the time?" Which was true, she visited us about once a week, always giving you a complimentary ride down the road.

"It's going to be winter soon and you're telling me yourself all the time that it's not safe." I could hear something in her voice bouncing off her guarded tone.

"How much are you getting for it?" I was trying to sound casual, as if money meant the same in our different worlds.

"Don't know, maybe four or five."

"But that's nothing and you won't be mobile anymore."

Not for the first time, I wished I could swallow my words back. There were still so many moments when I lost my footing, when I forgot that my normal was not her normal, when I made assumptions that were solely based on my world.

She said nothing for a while. I decided to dive in, "Do you need the money?"

"Yes," she said in a hard, defensive tone.

At this point I knew with absolute certainty that what I would say next could make or break our friendship. I could so easily be dismissive or patronising or even embarrassingly charitable, like giving a few rand and a fake smile to the homeless person begging at a traffic light.

Or I could just stop trying so hard to be right all the time.

"Is there something I can do to help?" I pressed the phone hard to my ear, trying to hold on to her.

"I can't talk about this right now. Let's talk another time, I have to go." Her voice was compressed and faint, like something hard and heavy was pressing down on her chest making it difficult to breathe.

With that she was gone.

I couldn't tell if she was angry or crying or in an area with bad cellphone reception.

I didn't know what to do.

After a few minutes of spooning down my cold soup and staring at the trees outside my window, I tried again.

Please talk to me. What is going on with you? I texted.

Almost immediately her answer appeared, *I am OK, just having a bit of a tough time at home. I'll come visit another time.*

She lived with her mother and younger brother, whom I knew she had had to support since her mother was retrenched from a managerial position in one of the big oil companies a few months back.

To keep her on the phone, I asked, *Are you at home right now?*

Yes.

Can I do anything? Please don't think I am trying to patronise you, I really want to help.

I could see that she was typing but nothing appeared. After a few minutes, I finally got an answer, *I don't think you are patronising. But it's hard for me to talk about. Nobody knows.*

I answered without thinking, *You don't need to tell me anything, if you don't want to. But at least let me help you out. If it's money you need, I can transfer into your account and we never have to talk about it again. Nobody needs to know.*

When I didn't hear back after a minute I tried again, *Or is it something else?*

More time passed. The typing and retyping again, before her answer appeared.

Thank you.

I waited for something more, but nothing came.

So what can I do? Would R4000 help? I asked.

Waiting again. Then, *Yes, that would help.*

I let out a big sigh, part relief, part worry. The new terrain of money could swallow us up and spit us out again, estranged and yet bound by dynamics of power and need.

I was determined to not mess this up. Not quite sure how though …

Do you want to text me your account details?

When her next text came, my vision blurred for a moment as I tried to make sense of what I saw, ***We haven't eaten in three days.***

Before I could think about it, I called her.

She picked up immediately.

"Hi," her normal, matter-of-fact voice.

"I can be at your house in twenty minutes; we can go from there to the shops." I was clear then what needed to be done, in full organising mode. Just quite how I was going to find her house in Gugulethu (I had only ever been to her aunt's place around the corner), and how I was going to manage driving around unmarked streets in a township area, when I tried my best to avoid playdates in unknown parts of Constantia, I had no idea.

"No, it's fine," she said, "I have Vuyelwa's car, should be enough petrol to get to you, we can go to Pick n Pay your side."

"OK," I agreed, relieved, "see you in a bit."

"All right, bye."

I checked the time, it was just after two. You would be back around five, which left us enough time to go shopping and for her to leave without you noticing her visit and asking uncomfortable questions.

I grabbed my bag and my car keys and waited outside. When I saw her driving up our road, I started the car and reversed out of our driveway. She parked opposite our gate and got in.

"Hi." We pecked each other on the cheek as I drove off.

"That was quick," I offered.

"Yes, no traffic for once."

"Do you want to go to Pick n Pay or somewhere else?" I asked.

"No, Pick n Pay is fine."

The rest of the way we didn't speak. I had no words for what I was feeling. I wanted to ask her so much. How could this happen? Why was there nobody in her life she felt she could talk to or ask for help? How was it possible for a family not to eat for three days without anybody noticing? Of course I knew it happened all the time. People suffered worse every day. Just not in my world.

Never in my world.

So I didn't say anything.

We parked in the underground garage just opposite the entrance of the new, expanded Pick n Pay, the size of a soccer field. I pushed the trolley and she directed me through the aisles. We systematically collected the necessities for a small family: milk, margarine, bread, vegetables, fruits, tea, sugar … Every so often I stopped and suggested something: *does your brother like Nutella (sure), maybe some sausages (only chicken), how about orange juice (let's get Oros rather).*

We finished off with toilet paper, soap, washing powder and dishwashing liquid, and then we waited at the tills.

She chatted to one of the cashiers who said something to her in isiXhosa. When I asked, she replied in a flat voice, "She asked me if you're my boss and why I am working on a Saturday."

"Did you tell her we're just friends?"

"Yep."

That explained the curious stares of the surrounding packers and other cashiers, laughing and calling out to each other over rows of tills.

A guy kept staring at her and I wanted to say something rude to him, but didn't.

When she eventually noticed him, she smiled and they shook hands. It turned out he was an old friend from school, now working at Pick n Pay customer services. He too looked at me curiously. As we left the shop, I felt weighed down by the hopelessness of it all.

Back at the house we moved the bags from my boot to hers. It was just before four and I asked her to come in for a cup of tea.

As we sat next to each other on the sofa, both staring into our cups, flashbacks of our nights spent talking ran through my mind, like long-ago memories of happier times. I was worried that I had already lost her, that the burden of my easy life compared to her daily struggles had finally ripped apart the delicate fabric of our friendship and there was no coming back from the fatal blow of my charity.

"How is your brother?" I asked inadequately.

"OK." She shrugged her shoulders. I could feel the movement against my arms. She shrugged again, then her face sank into her hands and I realised she was shaking with silent sobs. I felt clumsy and oppressive as I pressed her against me and she turned away from me, like I was trespassing on her grief. We sat awkwardly for a while.

A car approached and I strained my ears for the creaking of the gate, hoping you wouldn't burst in. The car drove past and the only sound in the room was her muffled, dry sobbing, like somebody suffocating.

"I am so sorry," I whispered.

She rubbed her hands over her face in a rough impatient gesture and sat up. My arm fell to my side.

"It's OK," she said, "it's just been a few hard days. I'll be fine."

She got up. "I'd better be going, my mum is probably wondering where I am."

I stood up too and followed her to the door. I opened the door for her. She left without looking back.

I was relieved she didn't feel the need to thank me.

26

Is She Your Madam?

It had been over a year into the dialogue group. I was struggling getting to the suburbs for our sessions because of finances. It was a difficult time for my family then. My mother had been out of work for about two years, and I couldn't find a job, which meant we could not pay the bond for the house. I was able to make some money here and there, but things got so bad we were struggling to even put food on the table. We knew we could not turn to family members because they had for years relied on my mother to support them. I was thinking about leaving the dialogue group. Their lives seemed so far removed from my reality.

Your mum had noticed I wasn't quite myself as we had spent some time together outside the sessions. She messaged to check how I was doing; how things were going; and if she could help in any way. We had not eaten for two days when I received this text. I cried after reading it as I was already in a bad space. I could not talk to my mother, as I could not imagine the pain she was going through. How does a mother deal with not being able to provide for her children? How awful must it feel for a mother to see her children hungry and not be able to do anything about it? **Going through a difficult time at the moment but I will be fine,** *I responded after some time. She kept messaging and pushing for me to open up to her. I felt embarrassed and ashamed because of our situation and did not want her to think less of me; I felt that letting her into my life would change our relationship. She and* *most people in my life knew me to be this strong black woman who spoke well and was (in their heads, not like the other black girls) in control of her life. I felt sharing with her would make me look like the typical poor black girl who is in need of help, she my white saviour, and I would eventually be her charity case. I would be the story she used to show what a good person she was and how she was not a racist. Sharing such information with her would block all possibility of us ever having a normal relationship.*

She kept pushing for me to open up to her. I did not understand why she was so persistent. White friends I had known for years – white friends who referred to me as a close friend – did not even know where I lived. I could not make sense of why a white person would be so invested in wanting to know what was happening in my life. I eventually opened up to her with tears running down my face and after a lot of hesitation responded with, **It is a really bad time for my family and I right now, things are really bad financially, we haven't eaten for two days.**

Please let me help. Can I drive to you and we go to Pick n Pay for you to get whatever you and your family need for the month? *she responded.*

I sat there for what seemed like hours reading this text over and over again. She sent another text, **Or we can do whatever is easiest for you.** *I sat in bed, still with tears running down my eyes, thinking about what this would do to my dignity and our relationship. She kept sending messages and calling but I would not pick up because I did not know what I would say to her. She sent another message,*

You need help; I have the money to help you. Please let me help.

I drove very slowly to meet her at her house. I thought about turning back, dreading the inevitable awkwardness. What was I going to say to her? What was she going to say to me?

She came outside as I was parking at her gate. I was relieved. I didn't know if I could handle putting on a brave face for one more person. We hugged and drove together to the mall. We spoke

149

about everything except what was happening, as if we had made a pact to avoid the topic. There were three conversations going on in the car: the one conversation was between us, the other in my head, and another in your mum's head. I wondered what she was thinking. I wondered if she had lost respect for me or thought less of me. Would she still want me to be around you? What form would our relationship take after this? Would we have a friendship?

"Who is this white lady you are with, is she your madam?" one of the cashiers asked in isiXhosa.

"What did she say?" your mum asked.

I was trying to think of something else to say, anything but what the cashier had actually said, because this would force us to deal with the elephant in the room. To my disappointment, I could not come up with anything and told her what the cashier said.

"Jeepers, hey, as if we can't be anything but a madam and her servant," she responded.

I dropped her back home and we didn't speak of this again for a long while.

After a couple of weeks of casual conversations, I went to your house for dinner. We chatted, we laughed, we connected, but there was some discomfort from my side. I was aware of my every move around her, always wondering what your mum was thinking and at times what I was doing sitting at this woman's dinner table. I found myself having to think through things before sharing with her. I felt my life was so different from hers that I had to pick and choose what to share with her, and the things I did share I had to repackage differently to how I shared with a black friend. Being around her made me feel I had had too much drama in my life.

But I stayed – and if I am honest, you were the main reason I didn't run away. By the time I realised just how uncomfortable and complicated a friendship with a white middle-class woman could be, I had already formed a special bond with you two (Nene wasn't born yet). You had become a part of my life and I couldn't imagine you growing up without me, and for me to not know the adults you would become one day.

You, Lele, remind me in many ways of myself when I was your age. You cover up your self-doubt and shyness in a bubbly chattiness, not giving the other person a chance to ask you any questions that might be uncomfortable, and drill them instead about anything and everything that comes to your mind (do you have a boyfriend, what car do you drive, where do you live, what was it like when you were at school ...). As far as you were concerned I was your Tumi and came to visit you; your Mum and I would have to take our time once you were in bed.

Both of us battle to articulate our feelings in a language that most people would understand. We connect and understand each other without words. I know that you know that I love you, that somehow you receive my love. I also know that you love me to bits even though these words would never come out of your mouth.

Our connection happens with us spending time together, talking nonsense and just soaking up each other's presence.

One of my favourite memories is when, a few years back, you had a huge fight with your mum and I just happened to call at that very instant. Your mum passed the phone on and all I heard was, Tumi, come and get me out of here, come fetch me now. I didn't ask any questions, just told you when I would be there and we drove back to my place without talking much. I knew you were upset but I also knew not to ask. Back at my house we curled up on the sofa, watched episode after episode of "Man vs. Child" and ordered Nqaba around, who brought food, drinks and blankets.

That night we slept in the big bed as you decided you didn't want to be alone and when we woke up we finished our episodes of "Man vs. Child" before I took you home again. That's our relationship in a nutshell, we get each other, what we have is perfect for us and doesn't have to make sense to anybody else.

Kal, you remind me of the man I married. You can be stubborn as hell. Nothing and no one can move or sway you. Once you make up your mind, you dig your heels in and settle like a mountain. You are also the kindest, warmest, most loving person I know.

When I met you, I did not understand how a child could have so much wisdom. I have many wonderful memories with you but the one that always stands out is when I accidentally referred to you by the wrong name (you had just decided to change your name). As I was still apologising, you reached out to me, touched my shoulder and said, "It's OK Tumi, don't be hard on yourself. It is sometimes hard to change something that you are used to and have been doing for a long time. Just keep trying, you will get it right." I almost burst into tears when you said that but had to contain myself because crying on the shoulder of a seven year old is not supposed to be OK. I was blown away by your response, blown away by how reflective you were and by the person that you are. You are able to be yourself in this hostile world in a way that I am at times not brave enough to be.

The first time I met you, Nene, was at the home you were staying at the time. I came with your mum and dad on one of their visits before they could finally take you home. The moment you saw me next to your mum, you came charging at me, like the cutest little crab, pincers outstretched, pinching me as hard as you could, your face serious, eyes scrunched up in concentration. You had a fierce pinch, and you were determined not to let me anywhere near you. For the entire visit I had to sit a few metres away from you and watch you play by yourself or with your mum. When it was time to go again, you pinched me goodbye.

Not much has changed in the last four years really – you still come charging at me whenever you see me, almost toppling me over with a jump that ends in a hug that almost chokes me. You are fierce and determined in every way – knowing just what you need and how to ask for it (I need a hug, can I have a kiss, can somebody wipe my bum – this last one shouted at full volume a few times a day until people come running from wherever they are in the house to assist you).

You were so happy when I had Nhloso, because that meant you were not the littlest in the family anymore and had your own little person who would look up to you. I remember one day when *he could barely crawl, finding you and him sitting opposite each other on the carpet with you chanting at him over and over: penis, bum, poopoo, penis, bum, poopoo. When I asked you what you were doing, you said to me in the most serious voice, "Tumi, I am teaching him his first words." I laughed so much, I actually cried.*

In time, your mum and I found that we were actually quite similar in a lot of ways and shared the same views on so many things. We spent many late nights chatting until your dad would come downstairs in his big white robe and say, "Darling, are you going to come up at all?"

I found that my "no mess" friend had her own dramas to deal with. We both had serious daddy issues that still manifested themselves in different ways in our lives. We were both fierce women who in some ways were little girls who believed they were not enough to be loved just for being themselves.

She was no longer the other – she was someone I connected with and even came to love.

The moments of discomfort and difficulty did not end. What we represented – her whiteness and my blackness – was so prevalent, I did not know if we could survive it. She for some reason kept trying. I kept expecting it to all get too much for her. I waited for her to get to the point where she felt that navigating the complexities of our friendship was too much work and would just give up but she did not.

I kept waiting and she kept trying. She is now one of the closest people in my life. We still have difficult moments, but we are both invested in the relationship and trust that we have created a space where our friendship can hold such difficulties.

27

Navy

She woke with cold creeping up her legs. It was still dark
out and at first she didn't know where she was. There was a
familiar dread in her belly like a bad dream when somebody
is chasing her and she knows they will hurt her, but her
legs are like jelly and she can't run fast enough. She could
make out grey shapes in the room: the bulk of a wardrobe
and a dresser on opposite walls and a darker rectangle in the
middle like a toothless yawn, which meant someone must
have come in late at night and left the door open. There
was the faint aroma of Johnson & Johnson baby powder
mixed with the sharp tang of something chemical, which
reminded her of the spray her aunt used every morning
(*Revlon, it will make you unforgettable*), and that's when she
remembered, she was back at her aunt's and uncle's house.

She called them aunt and uncle, but they made no bones
about how they felt about her; she was an intruder, someone
who did not belong, much too dark and skinny to be one
of them. They called her "darkie" or "navy" and laughed in
her face like she should find it funny too. Her colour was

like a dirt stain on the family linen that couldn't be washed out. So she made herself invisible or at least tried not to be any trouble. She didn't want to move again.

She could hear her uncle's snores and her aunt's feathery wheezes from the big bed above her mattress. Her cousin beside her moaned in his sleep and rolled over, taking a good portion of the blanket with him so that more cold air seeped in. She sat up, holding on to the corner of their blanket and folded her body into it, away from the wet spot, careful not to wake him. She watched the dark passage as she waited for the rest of the house to come to life.

The outside noises grew louder, as if there was a storm brewing: the rhythmic clatter of something metal against wood, probably a loose sheet from a nearby roof flapping in the wind; the bark of a dog accompanied by the rattle of a chain, as if he teared at it with each hacking bark, forever trying to get away; another dog howled from further away; somebody shouted outside their window; somebody else, a woman, screamed or laughed.

Still she didn't move.

She waited for her cousin to get up so she could drag the mattress out of the house and stack it at the usual spot against the wall before anybody would notice the wet patch. If she got caught, there would be lots of shouting and nasty smirks until the whole neighbourhood knew she had wet the bed again. Sometimes it wasn't even her. But she never defended herself, there was no point; nobody would believe her and the price for speaking her mind, she had learned long ago, was too high. Her granny would take her side, then the fighting would start and next thing, their bags would be outside and they would have to find another house, another set of aunts and uncles to take them in, their eyes narrow and hard with resentment.

Her granny loved her like nobody else. When she looked at her with that big smile that made her face shine and the skin around her eyes crinkle as if she had seen something beautiful and special, Tumi felt all the knots in her tummy melt away. Her granny called her Nomakholwa (*ye of faith*) and made it no secret that Tumi was her favourite. When she was well, she cooked for Tumi and washed and ironed her clothes so she looked proper, like she was from a good family. If Tumi had one wish, it would be for her and her granny to live in their own house, away from people, just the two of them, forever safe and happy.

From inside the house she could hear talking as ghost-like shapes moved past the open door. Somebody put the big pot of porridge on the stove with a bang and a screech, and the outside tap spit and coughed.

Her granny was not at home this morning. Once a month, on pay day, she took Tumi along at dawn to spend the morning in a long queue outside the grant office, and when it was finally their turn, she counted out the notes and coins and handed over her share "for the house" before she disappeared.

Tumi normally went looking for her in the evenings before it got dark and when she couldn't find her, or the old woman refused to come home with her, she tried again the next morning. She usually found her wandering around a few streets away from the shebeen, slurring words and falling over every few metres, with a bunch of neighbour-hood kids swarming around her like flies. They laughed and prodded at her with sticks and grubby fingers, jumping and screeching with mock fear every time the old woman swiped a wobbly hand at them like she was trying to catch cockroaches in the dark. It was easier to get her home in the mornings, when she had been drinking all night and didn't know who she was or where she lived. She allowed Tumi to lead her away from the screeching kids, and Tumi would put her to bed, making sure the blanket was pulled up to her chin and that she was lying on her side so she wouldn't choke in her sleep.

Tumi would have been happy to stay with her granny to watch her sleep and make sure she had a bowl of soup or porridge when she woke up. But the adults didn't allow children in the house during the day. All the small ones, who didn't yet attend school, got sent out after breakfast to play until dark. Sometimes, somebody made them jam and peanut butter sandwiches for lunch, but most days there was nobody home to remember.

Tumi hated jam and peanut butter sandwiches almost as much as she hated the hungry feeling gnawing at her insides like a fat mean rat. Most days she didn't even bother to go back to the house to check if there was lunch. She preferred spending the day with the neighbourhood boys, who had a grudging respect for her. She could outrun even the fastest of them and show them a trick or two about kicking a ball. She had also made friends with the shy boy from the neighbourhood spaza, who got them cool stuff, like a real ball and lots of TV games, which they played in the back of the shop. The room was dark and stuffy and smelled of dust and greasy sausages (fat Russians, five rand a pop) that made her stomach turn.

Often they made their own lunch over a fire in some-body's backyard, mostly stolen potatoes boiled in a tin, and sometimes a half-burned pigeon caught with an empty jam jar held up with a stick and a piece of string. The meat had a weird smell, like something rotten, but it tasted OK, a bit like chicken, and the glamour of a self-made lunch beat peanut butter sandwiches any day.

Some days they played Make Believe: their favourite game was to pretend they were white and lived in a mansion. Tumi had never seen a white mansion but her granny used to clean in one and told her about polishing shiny gold-coloured taps with endless streams of hot water, scrubbing bathtubs the size of a small room, and sitting on gleaming white toilets (when the madam was out) that washed your bum while you were doing your business. She talked about hanging up washing in endless green gardens amongst trees heavy with orange and yellow fruit that nobody picked, and flowers so bright and shiny you couldn't look at them directly; she whispered about children who came home from school to their own nanny who made them milk with honey and cooked them whatever they wanted for their lunch. Later the nannies would take the children to parks with climbing trees, rainbow-coloured jungle gyms and musical ice-cream trucks parked outside the gates, or they played in their own rooms full of toys and dolls and glittery storybooks. All the white kids had cupboards full of clothes, so they could wear new things every day. In a white mansion even the dogs had beds and clothes and three meals a day.

What Tumi loved most about these stories were the colours. She listened with her eyes closed, imagining the shiny golds and glowing greens, almost tasting the juicy yellows and oranges and pinks like pieces of fruit on her tongue. But when she opened her eyes again, everything around her seemed even more drained, nothing but the tired grey of clothes washed over and over and over again; grey streets and grey houses, hunched together like a bunch of drunks trying to keep each other up; grey piles of rubbish blown about in the never-ending wind; swirling grey clouds of dust; grey pieces of plastic stuck to barbed wire fences.

Whenever the colours left, fear came creeping back, filling the empty spaces inside of her with shards of ice. Invisible eyes watching her sleep, faceless men preying on her from behind windows and on street corners, waiting, always waiting, for what she was too afraid to imagine.

Her cousin finally sat up, glared at her, and jumped off the mattress as if bitten by a snake.

Tumi sighed and started folding up the blanket.

Time to start her day.

28

White Pain

We didn't speak about our shopping trip for the longest time, Tumi and I, but instead of driving us apart, as I had feared it would, we found a bond somewhere in its aftermath. It was not the euphoric high of early friendship, of finding somebody "just like me"; this felt more like we were lone survivors crawling from underneath the debris of a train crash or emerging from a collapsed building, connected to each other by an experience too raw to put into words.

Also, you already loved her and she you. She had become your Tumi within a few months of meeting you. You were the main reason, I know now, she stuck it out with me despite her doubts and fears. Especially Lele was smitten, making sure I knew I was just the background noise every time your beloved Tumi came to visit. Sometimes we dropped you at school together after she had spent the night and you proudly held her hand instead of mine, presenting her as your Mama's friend to your pale classmates. "Black and white, how are they friends?" they whispered to each other, more curious and confused than dismissive, only mirroring what they knew about their four-year-old worlds.

We would make our way to the child sized tables amongst giggles and stares, perched on tiny chairs, and help you finish your morning sewing or weaving as you glowed under her attention. On those days she got the hugs and goodbye kisses and the final wave through the window, while you watched me out of the corner of your eye for a reaction. So I pretend-wiped my eyes and made to grab you back from her, which made you giggle and hold on even tighter. "No Mama, go away ... MY Tumi," hiding your face in Tumi's jacket so I wouldn't see your glee.

"My Tumi," I said and hugged you both, barely breathing for happiness. Today, many years later, you still ask me out of the blue, just to double check, "Who is your best friend?"

"Tumi."

Sometimes you ask her, and when she says "your mama" you move on to the next subject, as if the question was never important in the first place. The three of you became the bridge over which we found each other over and over again when life was pulling us apart.

On the day of the shopping trip I had stepped into the shadow of somebody else's experience, felt the light around me change, the ground beneath my feet shift, and lost my footing. I knew this was my chance to pause and simply feel what I needed to feel: disoriented, confused and yet connected to another.

The next time we saw each other we sat on opposite sides of a chair circle on Jan's upstairs balcony, balancing plates with homemade salads, Woollies roast chicken and bread on our laps as people gathered for our monthly dialogue meeting. It had been a hot autumn day but as soon as the sun disappeared behind the mountain, the air grew chilly and Jan offered blankets and wine. There was cheering and laughter coming from the food table, where Deirdre and Di rehashed a university social they had both attended. Deirdre was still relatively new to the group, presented to us like a shiny trophy a few months earlier by Thando, who took great pride in her learned friend. Deirdre was deeply and apologetically white South African, with a tendency to burst into lectures and leave meetings early because the issues we discussed made her "feel traumatised and unable to sleep". The relief I felt each time she didn't pitch for a meeting and my irritation whenever she did show up had me doubt my motives and intentions. Hoping to overcome my sentiment and to grow as a person, but mostly because I lacked the verbal proficiency to back up my diffuse feelings, I tried my best to avoid eye-rolling and hand-flicking every time she opened her mouth.

When Di and Deirdre had proposed to facilitate this evening's session, "White Pain", I expected our conversations to turn some treacherous corners, but I could not have anticipated what was coming. I don't think any of us did. We were ripped apart at the seams with no tools at our disposal to stitch us back together.

It all started harmlessly enough with Deirdre handing out sheets of paper, asking us to take a few deep breaths, cleanse our minds of the clutter of the day, grab a pen and free-associate for five minutes to the word "white". The classroom atmosphere took me back to all the reasons I have always hated groups. I wondered at my failure to overcome or even understand my belligerence in the face of her professional airs. I had to fight a strong impulse to flick spitballs around the room.

Instead, I took a pen from the glass jar on the floor and started writing: WHITE, big fat summer clouds, Snow White and the Seven Dwarfs, Mummel my first rabbit ... I ran out of steam and looked at the bowed heads around me, my need to fit in and be liked at odds with my instinct to stamp my foot and *not* write the words that hung like neon signs from the rooftops around us: white is right, beauty and innocence, guilt, privilege, superiority.

"Time is up," said Deirdre. "Who wants to share?"

I folded my paper and leaned back in my chair, making it clear (I hoped) that it wouldn't be me. Next to me Kate had draped one of the blankets around us both and I felt a little less fragmented, soothed by her gesture of uncomplicated affection.

In the months following my dinner party, we had stumbled upon our friendship with mutual surprise, like looking across a room full of strangers and finding a childhood friend, whom I last saw when I was seven. We started bonding over styling our girls' hair. I became her apprentice, eagerly taking notes as she tweaked and changed her homemade moisturisers, detanglers and hair foods on a weekly basis. We hunted for diverse toys and books online and in stores all over the city, winning arguments with those who tried to sell us animal picture books as valid alternatives to stories with black heroes and princesses. We went for long walks on the mountain or along the promenade, trying out intimacies like wearing each other's favourite clothes, cackling like a pair of witches. I had talked her into joining our group a few months ago, just before Deirdre made her first appearance, and had felt hypervigilant ever since, as if it were my responsibility to make sure we did not waste her time. This of course was at the core of my irritation: my fear that she would come to see me as just another white girl covering up my insecurities and unprocessed entitlement with layers of jargon and alibi-friendships.

Having her next to me, cocooned in our blanket, I felt comforted and intensely uncomfortable at the same time, as if this was my moment to prove my worthiness, but my mind went blank.

"Phew," Jan let out a sigh, "this was difficult for me."

Others nodded their consent. Tumi was staring into the distance, not even pretending to be interested.

"What came up for me was mainly negativity around

whiteness, all the poisonous stuff. It made me feel ashamed and guilty," Jan continued, her voice low, almost a whisper.

"Can you read us some of your words?" Deirdre switched from chirpy to professionally calm and looked kindly at Jan.

"Sure ..." Jan sighed again.

"White is right, angels, innocence, white superiority, guilt, shame." She paused, tucked a strand of blonde hair behind her ear and wiped the back of her hand across her forehead as if to rub away unpleasant thoughts. "I don't know, it's so difficult to talk about. We've always centred black experiences in this group and somehow focusing on whiteness feels a bit wrong. It is like everybody always centres whiteness and we should be doing something else."

Some nods. Tumi took a swig of wine, briefly met my eyes and looked away again. A fork clattered onto the wooden floorboards.

"I can hear how difficult this is for you," counselled Deirdre, "but we all decided to talk about this today, and maybe it is a good thing to switch the focus for once. Does anybody else want to share?"

"I'll go." Thando tossed her braids and read from her paper, "Beauty, wealth, white knight in shining armour." She giggled and flicked a mischievous look into the circle, "Did I tell you I just found my blue-eyed prince by the way?"

"No way!" Di exclaimed. Deirdre high-fived her.

"I'll tell you later," promised Thando to the rest of us before she carried on. "What stands out for me most is how whiteness is the standard that *others* me everywhere I go. I can't even be in a bar or restaurant in the area I live in (which is mostly white) without being made to feel out of place and like an intruder."

"Well, most people in this country don't have the problem of how to fit in at a white restaurant, they struggle to find food." Tumi's voice was sharp and unforgiving.

"I know I am privileged," said Thando with a quick

sideways glance at Tumi, "but this is my reality and maybe we should start to address the intersectionality between class and race instead of always focusing on race."

"Let's maybe focus back on the topic of whiteness?" Deirdre put a question mark behind her request but to me she sounded bossy. "Does anybody else want to share their writing? Di?" She looked at her co-facilitator to get the session back on track.

"Not really." Di shrugged her shoulders, sending an apologetic smile her way. "But I was just thinking about a story a friend told me, who came to South Africa as an aid worker a few years ago," she continued. "She said that her whole life she had been a human being first, comfortable in her skin, but the moment she got to South Africa, she was constantly reminded that she was white, and therefore guilty of being a racist. She said she felt black people were being hostile and judged her because of her skin colour. She actually cried when she told me her story and I think she went back home soon after."

"Wow," Thando sighed, "this is so sad."

"I am wondering if it is maybe more her feeling guilty, coming as a white privileged person to this country and becoming aware of her privilege, rather than people really judging her?" Vuyelwa offered, her voice calm and reasonable as always.

"Well, I can tell you from my own experience that I get judged for my whiteness quite a lot at my workplace," Di said. "Lots of my coworkers and my boss are black and they often lump me in with the racists, even though they know that I am married to a black man."

"Do you have an example?" Vuyelwa wanted to know.

"Yes I do, actually. When I was offered a job at this mainly white company, which lots of people perceive as racist and backwards, somebody at my work said to me, why don't you apply, you fit right in?"

"OK, that was maybe harsh to hear, but have you considered that they were referring to you being white without accusing you of being racist?" Vuyelwa said.

"It didn't feel like it was harmless," Di replied.

"I think your point is, Vuyelwa," Deirdre said, "that we can only speculate in this instance whether it is just Di's perception or if somebody is actually implying she is racist. We can't know that for sure, but maybe I can give you another example, something that happened to me recently."

I sat up at that. Deirdre offering something personal was a rare thing.

"So when I walked along the promenade in Sea Point a while back, there was this group of black men standing on the side of the pavement, glaring at me, and as I passed them I heard them say 'white bitch' and other things I don't want to repeat. This was clearly just because of the colour of my skin; they didn't know anything about me and actually made me feel violated and afraid to walk there in the future." She paused, clearly struggling with her emotions, then added in a choked voice, "I don't want to live in fear just because I happen to be white and my parents have always warned me of 'black danger' back in the days and did nothing to fight Apartheid."

There was a moment of silence. Tumi threw me a warning look, as if I was about to roll my eyes. I felt cold and a little ashamed that Deirdre's tears didn't move me like they should.

"Wow, thank you for sharing this Deirdre," said Thando. "I think I understand for the first time what white people are going through."

Deirdre nodded at her and they touched hands for a moment.

With a sudden movement, the blanket fell off my shoulder as Kate straightened up in her seat and took a deep breath. Then she spoke in a quiet voice which grew in volume and intensity as she seemed to rise above us all, lost in a space all by herself.

"I don't know about you but I fail to see the relevance of what you are recounting set against what my people have been going through for centuries and still suffer to this day. I fail to see the relevance of a white woman's pain when she realises for the first time in her life at the age of maybe thirty-five or forty and after having lived for that entire time in blissful oblivion, that she is actually white and privileged and that she is part of a racist system whether she likes it or not. I fail to see the relevance of this self-indulgent pain in the light of my grandmother's, my mother's, my own and my daughter's pain as we get told from when we first play in sandpits with white kids that we have to be the servants and slaves and can never be princesses or queens because we are black and our hair is ugly. I fail to see the relevance of a white woman's decision to move back to the safety of her white country the moment she feels uncomfortable amongst black people, or a white woman feeling threatened walking in her white neighbourhood because there are angry black men standing on the pavement, when she can call the police or Armed Response, and they are in all likelihood going to arrest them and protect her and not the other way round. I fail to see the relevance of a white woman's pain because she feels unfairly judged as being part of a system of white supremacy that protects her at every corner, when my people are nowhere safe from abuse and violence because there are no safe spaces for blackness anywhere in this world. I just totally fail to see the relevance here tonight in this group – "

Her voice was shaking with anger or tears or both and she abruptly stopped, got up and went into the house, leaving behind a stunned silence.

I thought about following her, but found myself unable

to move. It felt like I had just witnessed an entire building crumble in front of my eyes, and I had yet to understand the danger we were all in. Jan got up and followed her instead. The rest of us continued to sit in silence.

Then Deirdre spoke, "Well, we actually all agreed to talk about white pain in this session so should we get back to our topic?"

"What?" I exploded, before I could think, "I cannot believe that you can sit here calmly after what has just happened and actually want us to get back to the programme. I don't have words for how I feel at the moment; devastated, humbled, destroyed, ashamed don't even touch it. There could be so much we can learn from this but you just want to get back to a prescribed agenda?"

I heard my voice shake and I stopped. This wasn't about me. I looked around in the hope somebody else was going to take this up.

An almost imperceptible nod from Tumi.

Vuyelwa stared across the rooftops.

Thando looked at Di with bright eyes, and Di finally jumped in, "I am sorry but I agree with Deirdre. For almost two years we have only ever spoken about black pain and black experiences and the one time we agree to talk about white pain, the conversation gets hijacked by black pain again. I don't think this is fair at all."

New anger rose in my throat. I sat and stewed some more.

"Maybe we need to acknowledge at this point that all relevant spaces are white spaces in this world and that as a norm white voices are being heard and white feelings attended to at the expense of black voices and black feelings everywhere; maybe we need to stop here and acknowledge this first." Vuyelwa was calm like a judge. I could tell this was the soothing voice she used when she was forced to explain herself to white people, so they wouldn't feel threatened by her black anger.

"I agree with Di," Thando said. "We have been talking about racism and black pain for years, and I for one would like to talk about intersectionality and black privilege."

Jan came back into the room and sat down. She looked flushed and scattered like she too was about to cry. I could see Kate standing by the door; she looked at me and I realised she was not coming back. Something passed between her and Tumi and then Tumi got up and said she needed to go.

As she was staying with me for the night, I took this as my prompt to get up too. The others looked on – hurt, hostile and stunned.

Jan held out her hands pleading with us, "Maybe we should all leave it at that for now as emotions are clearly running high. Maybe we should all go home and think about what happened here this evening and not forget what we are all about as a group."

"Should we make a date for our next meeting?"

"It's always the first Thursday of the month, right?" Deirdre said.

"I'll email everyone," offered Di.

We mumbled goodbyes, Jan got up to hug us, and then Tumi, Kate, and I were standing outside Jan's house, looking at each other like we had just come out of an accident.

"Debrief at my house," Kate specified.

"I'll go with her, meet you there," Tumi said to me and I got into my car and followed them the five-minute drive to Kate's house. We got there at the same time. Kate led the way and switched on a light in the lounge. It was cold and she offered to make tea. Tumi didn't want any and neither did I. Kate brought out an open bottle of wine from the kitchen, three glasses, and a packet of chips. We clinked glasses. Tumi and I perched on the edge of a two-seater couch and Kate sat down opposite us. We all took a breath. Then they started.

I sat in silent awe as they finished each other's sentences, hands flying into high-fives, eyes sparking with anger, voices erupting with laughter, ripping the evening apart and putting it back together until an entirely new picture emerged in front of my eyes. It felt like sitting in a darkened room at the optometrists, trying to decipher out-of-focus objects projected onto a wall and then as if by magic everything becoming crystal clear with one simple change of lenses.

I was not even sure anymore that I was invited to this conversation or if they had simply forgotten about me as they drew a map of an unknown country, between crumbs of chips and half-empty wine glasses. As I witnessed my friends' unfiltered anger and heard them talk about white tears, white fragility, the privilege of owning spaces, being the centre of attention and dominating narratives, my lens switched from safely empathising with blackness to a clear view of an all-pervasive whiteness. Maybe that was the moment when I realised how my whiteness and what it represented was fused to my identity and how it made me harmful and dangerous to the black people in my life and even to my own children.

I sat in shock and mourning as our dialogue group lay dead between us, the postmortem executed and the body cobbled back together for a swift burial.

29

White Pain, Take Two

If I could erase that session from my mind, I would. It was horrible. I do not remember the details but I remember what I felt.

For a long while the dialogue space felt like a white space, a space where whites were centred and blacks had to bend themselves into pretzels to accommodate white people's feelings. We could not use our full range of emotions, even after provocation, because it might make the white people feel "attacked" or "judged". How my reaction might affect them seemed more important than me being able to express myself fully. I was not always able to articulate this feeling but it was one I was familiar with.

The dialogue group we had created to fight against racism had become like the model C school with mostly white kids that I had attended, preaching diversity, unity and all kinds of "wonderful" things but in everything that remained unspoken it was hostile to my wellbeing.

I learned to get by in high school and I suppose I learned to get by in the group as well ... until the white pain dialogue where the pushback was explicit and in our face. It felt like the white members used that session to let out all the anger they hid under the niceties and "dialogue ground rules". The first mistake was to name the session "white pain". The second mistake was having two whites facilitate the session. We had never had a session on "black pain". Yes, the pain of black people did come up in most if not all sessions but that was because of the society we live in and how it is still to this day structured against us. Everyone could express themselves, ask questions, and say what they thought. But in this particular session, we (the blacks) kept getting shut down, reminded that this was a "white pain" dialogue every time we tried to give context to some of the things the whites were saying. We were told not to make it about blacks. Our white members continued to talk about how they too were not allowed in a restaurant because they were dressed in dodgy clothes or how they experienced hate from blacks who wanted them to leave the country or called them a bitch while walking at the promenade. As I said, I don't really remember the stories. Their stories were valid and important – what annoyed and hurt me about them was that they were told in a way that nullified the stories we had shared, "We acknowledge your experience of racism, but ..."

I had spent months in conversations with these people and shared deep, personal stories that I thought somehow connected us to each other but in that moment, I might as well have been with strangers. I tried sitting back and listening for a while to try and understand them. I looked around the room to see if everyone else around me was losing their marbles. I remember seeing Kate holding on tightly to herself and your mama looking confused with her usual "what the hell" face. The more we tried to talk, the more our two facilitators pushed back harder like they had been holding their anger in for a while and this was their opportunity to let it out. At some point it got a bit much and Kate lost it. She was intense – the moment was raw and stopped everyone dead on their feet. Our facilitators had no chance to brush her off with "don't make this about blacks" like they had been doing before.

Kate let it all out. She spoke about her story in a deep and personal way. She spoke about her childhood experiences, her child's experiences, and how whiteness affected their lives. I saw myself in her story, I knew all about low self-esteem, aspiring to white beauty standards, and having everything around you affirm that you are less than. Seeing Kate in that moment of vulnerability touched me deeply and opened the floodgates to my childhood pain. I too started crying.

There was silence in the room. I thought that moment would allow us all to take a step back but something in our fellow whites did not allow them to take it. We were hit with another, "Yes, but …" and the conversation moved on like there wasn't someone in the room who had just broken down in front of us. When I think back I get angry at the white members of the group and I feel ashamed that I let them continue and allowed for Kate to be abused in that manner. I should have shut the conversation down; I should have stood up for her (for myself), but I didn't. I was immobilised by the pain I was feeling.

Kate declared she would never go back to group. I too had many reasons for not wanting to go back but I also felt I owed it to Kate not to go back and I didn't for a while.

30

The Meeting After

It took us weeks before we were ready to approach each other again as a group. Somebody sent an email to suggest a debrief session but responses were slow and reluctant. The dates didn't suit, the time wasn't right, too much to do at work, a child was sick; everybody, other than Kate, made excuses for their absence.

Tumi was about to move house and said she was too busy.

Vuyelwa wrote she wouldn't be able to attend for the time being because of work commitments.

Thandeka kept quiet on email but told Tumi she was never coming back; she said that after what happened, she needed healthy spaces with black women.

I pleaded with Kate to come to one last meeting, hoping she could make people understand what went wrong, but she said she had enough white fragility to deal with at work and that she had to do some self-care. She said she refused to be a token black educator and the group was a waste of her time.

I was mostly worried that with her and Tumi gone, it would be left to me to deliver their message of our failure and that I would do it badly. I also knew it was time for me to step up, to leave my safe corner and take a stand, however flawed and shaky it might be. We finally agreed on a date to meet at my house. It was only four of us, all white women.

Di brought a friend from Germany, who was volunteering in a South African orphanage or some other place of need for a few weeks, and who had expressed an interest in our process. She asked if she could be a silent observer.

We circled around bread and soup for a while, making small talk, the air thick with embarrassment and unasked questions as if we were distant work colleagues happening upon each other in a holding cell of drunk drivers.

When we ran out of safe topics and food, there was no more avoiding the elephant in the room. "Sjoe, where is everybody? It looks like it's only the four of us," Di observed.

"Yes, I don't think anybody else is coming," Jan said. "Tumi is moving, Thandeka is out of town working, and Vuyelwa texted me to say her daughter is sick," she added, with a "life-is-happening" shrug.

"Deirdre also said she couldn't make it, she sends her apologies," Di said. I stared hard at some spilled soup on the kitchen counter.

"So should we start?" I asked. I settled into a corner closest to the window so I could look out.

"Yes, let's get going. I don't think we need to have an opening circle, seeing there's so few of us." Jan sent a smile to our silent observer. "Damn, that was a tough session, last time," her voice wobbled with a forced laugh.

"Yes, it took me a really long time to get over it," Di said. "I felt really judged by what was said in the end. After all, we had agreed on the subject of white pain and then we were made to feel guilty for talking about it."

"I know what you mean," said Jan, "it felt very unsafe. I think we should have had outside facilitation for this session, as the subject of white pain is very raw for many of us. Also, seeing that most of us are not here tonight, it feels wrong to talk about what actually happened in too much detail, so maybe we should rather brainstorm about how we can make the dialogue space safe again?"

Di nodded her agreement. Her friend looked bored. From upstairs I heard giggles and splashing and Alan's monster-growls as he chased you from bath to bedroom. I wished this evening was over already and I could join in the bedtime routine and then zone out on reruns of *Friends*.

They all looked at me and I realised it was my turn to contribute. I felt my face heat up with what I was about to say.

"How can you sit here and pretend nothing much has changed, as if it is just an unfortunate coincidence that only we white women are here today and everybody else had 'other things going on'?" (I really did make the finger-curls for quotation marks in the air.)

"Is it only obvious to me that black women in this group had enough, because we failed them over and over again? At best, this dialogue is simply not useful to them. At worst, and I am thinking of our last meeting now, our group has become abusive and traumatising; we somehow managed to re-create a microcosm of the racist society we live in, where white people's feelings and insecurities take centre stage at the expense of black voices. We have been talking about this stuff for almost three years and this is what we are left with? A group of four white women whining about how we feel judged and hurt by this group and our solution is to yet again centre on our vulnerability and brainstorm about creating a safer space for us?"

My voice was too loud and my face too red; I knew I came across as aggressive and angry, but I couldn't stop.

"And talking about you feeling judged, why don't you come right out with it and tell it how it is: it is me you feel judged by, am I right? Since I am the only one loud and angry around here …"

There was a moment of silence. I took a breath and they looked at each other, as if they had anticipated my outburst and were silently agreeing on who was going to deliver their pre-formulated response. I didn't wait for it though.

"So my question to you is: *Why do you care?* What makes me so important or so powerful that my opinions or rather how I voice them can affect your safety? Sure, my feelings are often too obvious; when I speak, my anger shows or my guilt, and sometimes I roll my eyes or pull an annoying face. But we have known each other not only within this group but outside as friends; we sat at each other's tables for Christmases and birthdays – and this is what it boils down to? Me judging you and *making* you feel unsafe? What does it really mean, this concept of a safe space and no judgement? Isn't it just an excuse to avoid calling out each other's bullshit? If in your eyes it is judgement when I don't agree with you in a way that is palatable to you, when my voice is not quite "kumbaya" enough, when I get pissed off and frustrated, then yes, I probably have judged you all in recent times. But so what? Just tell me to shut up and calm down. There are many more important issues that we have been consistently suppressing with our unrealistic and entitled expectations of safety."

"I don't think you are – " Jan started.

"I'm not finished," I cut her off.

"Your expectation of a safe space is absurd and reeks of white entitlement. There has never been a safe space for black women in this group. They are expected to expose themselves, to open themselves up to our prodding, our doubts, our guilt, our insensitive questions or our self-indulgent wishes to be educated by them about how it feels to be black. So that at the end of the day we can pat ourselves on the back because we are doing such a good thing and we really, really care. But we have become a group of abusive voyeurs and what happened in our last session just proves my point."

I had to take another breath and this time Jan jumped in, two red spots on her cheeks, "Jeez, you think you are so much better than us, sitting pretty in your little clique with Kate and Tumi, excluding everyone else, because we are so far below you and you know it all …"

Jan took a shaky breath and looked at her fingers all twisted around each other in her lap. Her outburst was so out of character that I couldn't tell whether she was shaking with anger or trying to contain unacknowledged grief. It hit me how left out and hurt my friendships with Tumi and Kate must have made her feel. It had never occurred to me how much she wanted to be in on what we have, but simply didn't know how to join us.

Nobody spoke for a while, and I waited for her to look up so I could read her face. I wanted to tell her I was glad we were finally real with each other, and also sorry I was so absorbed by my own mission that I had excluded her, and that I had had no idea she felt that way.

But how could I not have known? Maybe I knew only too well and the glow of being on the inside for once in my life had turned into a gloat. I wanted to tell her that we needed to have that conversation, but not now.

She looked up, her features calm, her eyes scanning the room for safe places to settle. "And no, Martina," she said, her voice still a little husky, but sensible and reasonable, as if she were talking to a teenage daughter in the throes of a hormonal melt-down, "We don't think it is just you doing the judging – or you being at the centre of the issue. There is a whole lot more to this than you seem to understand or even want to acknowledge. This is not about you but about us as a group, about our initial intentions to dialogue and how we can get back to those and do better in future. If we don't respect each other's feelings and opinions, if we don't allow each other to be at different stages in this process, dialogue cannot happen, because people will feel unsafe and they will close up or get defensive. The essence of dialogue is not venting your anger and forcing your opinion down other people's throats, but engaging respectfully through enquiry instead of attacking one another."

I was thrown by her change of tack and the rightness of her statement made my eyes glaze over. But we were on familiar ground again and I was still up for the fight.

"You are right, dialogue ideally should be about mutual respect and enquiry, but if power is not equally distributed, then respect goes in one direction only and enquiry turns into abuse. We have wielded our white power by refusing to be vulnerable; by demanding safe spaces for ourselves; by guarding our fragile egos and carefully constructed identities. Meanwhile black women in this group are expected to open up about deeply traumatic and personal experiences; experiences which then get questioned and unpacked by white people according to a dialogue manual – that they invented – in so-called polite enquiry. Not only do we prod and question and exploit their experiences, we also tell them how to react towards us, how to express their feelings so they don't make us feel unsafe. We decide what is acceptable and what is not. If somebody does get angry, outraged, or frustrated, we are quick to call it judgement and demand calm reasoning before we deign to listen, or we change the subject altogether. Look where this has got us," I spread my hands and looked around me in mock surprise, "there is no one left to dialogue with."

Di straightened up from her slouch opposite me and threw me a look I couldn't read, a warning maybe, but I didn't give her a chance, "As white people in this group, it is high time we look beyond our egos, and expose all the tender spots we are trying so hard to hide: the white abuser of undeserved power, the racist that – maybe through no fault of our own – lives in all of us and expects to be pampered and talked to politely and calmly by the very same people we hurt. If we are not making ourselves vulnerable, and expose our own shit, we will never be in an equal space, dialogue will never happen and we might as well go home now. There, I am done."

I sank back into my corner of the couch, my face a burning mess, my armpits damp, and my words throbbing in my head like a migraine. I half-expected people to get up and go home, but we remained in place, unmoving.

Di eventually shifted in her armchair and uncurled her legs. A shadow crossed her eyes that made her look sad and tired. When she spoke, her usual matter-of-fact voice came out in a hoarse whisper, "I think I do that a lot. I try to stay on the outside of things and don't get too involved so I won't embarrass myself or make myself vulnerable. I do get now how this could be exploitative and even abusive towards the black women in our group."

She paused. Her eyes wandered around the room and then settled somewhere outside. The sunset had come and gone and the city lights were sparkling too festively for our sombre mood. Jan smiled at her but Di didn't notice.

"I don't know if I can stay in the group," she continued. "But I know that, if I do, I will have to bring myself in more."

Jan flinched, maybe alarmed at the thought that Di might also be leaving.

"I never thought about it this way," Jan started, her words drawn out and tentative as if practising a new language. "It didn't even occur to me that the way we white people interact in this group could be harmful to black people. I thought it was my right to stay distant and uninvolved, or that it was OK for white people to leave this space whenever it got too uncomfortable. I realise now that black women don't have that option … they can never take a break from racism …" her voice trailed off.

For a while nobody said anything, more of a contemplative pause than speechless hostility; we looked at each other again as we searched each other's faces for a new understanding.

"Can I say something?" Di's friend broke her vow of silence. I wanted to shout, "No!" I was afraid this moment would slip away from us before we could begin to see a new picture emerge.

Jan, diplomatic as ever, said, "Yes, of course, go right ahead."

The friend commented how this had been so interesting for her to witness, and how she would strongly advise us to invite an outside facilitator to the next meeting, and wow she hadn't even been aware of all the tensions between black and white people in South Africa, and thank you so much for allowing her to be a part of this.

Shut the fuck up, I thought. Di said "you're welcome" to her friend and the moment was gone.

I wish I could say that we found a new way forward that evening, that we learned from our mistakes, and slowly rebuilt our group with a new and improved understanding.

But we drifted for a while longer, avoiding meetings, barely keeping in touch, until one day we were thrown back together by an unexpected moment of notoriety, our fifteen minutes of fame.

31

The Twelve Apostles

"Martina, you need to speak to this lady here, apparently she can't find our reservation." Tumi was calling from The Twelve Apostles in Cape Town where I had booked a table at one of their restaurants for her and some friends and family a few hours earlier.

When she tried to book under her own (African) surname, she was told there was no table available for that evening. Smelling a racist rat, she had asked me to try with my "white voice" and European surname. Surprise, surprise, I got a booking, no problem. *Seven o'clock for eight guests? Certainly, Ma'am, have a lovely evening.*

We thought about just letting the reservation go – spending a sizeable amount of money being surrounded by glares and stares, because your skin colour doesn't match the décor, would not be anybody's idea of a nice evening out – but in the end Tumi's fighting spirit took over and they went anyway.

It was Saturday evening bath time, a few days after Christmas, and I was busy chasing you around the tub with washcloths and toothbrushes, the front of my t-shirt soaked, when I heard my phone buzz on the wooden stairs outside the bathroom. I didn't even check. Nobody ever called me. I much preferred the efficiency of texts over the protocol of how-are-yous and fine-thank-yous required to even get the briefest of messages across in a voice call.

But after a few seconds, it buzzed again and then a third time, and when I went to check, I saw Tumi's name on the display and answered.

I hadn't expected to hear her tales about her evening out in a racist restaurant until much later that night or the next day, but when she told me they were stuck at reception, I was lost for words.

"What?" I asked, hoping I misunderstood and she might be asking under what name I had made the reservation.

"She says you never booked, she can't find your name anywhere on their system," Tumi clarified.

"OK, let me speak to her." The moment my back was turned, you started a fight about some bath toy or other and I had to make eye contact and shake my free hand "shush" and "stay where you are" at you, while waiting for Tumi to hand over the phone to whoever was in charge.

"Hello, this is Janine speaking, how may I help you?" Her voice, effused with belligerence made a growl rise in the back of my throat.

"Hi, I booked a table for eight with you this morning under the name of Dahlmanns," I said in my best white voice, still pleasantly enough.

"Do you remember who took your reservation?" she asked me, newly alert, as if she had caught a whiff of something burning.

"No I don't, is there a problem?" I employed my no-nonsense-I'm-counting-to-three parenting tone.

"Ma'am, I am really sorry but we don't seem to find a reservation under your name."

"This is strange, since the person I spoke to this morning took my name and number and assured me a table would be available for my party at seven-thirty."

"Were you planning on joining the guests?" she asked, stalling.

"No, I wasn't, and I don't see how this is relevant, unless

your establishment is only open to white people?"

I heard a hiss or it might have just been static as she pondered the question for quite some time.

"I am sorry, Ma'am, there must be a misunderstanding," she eventually said.

"Oh really?" I sounded like I do when you are trying to convince me that our dog was responsible for the mess in the kitchen or stole the chocolate from the sweets drawer while hiding your sticky fingers behind your backs. "A misunderstanding, huh?" (*Let me see your hands, missy.*)

"I think it more likely that you are under orders not to allow black people into your restaurant and you'd better find me a manager right this moment with a really great apology or I will go public with this." I wished I didn't sound so flustered. I was under no illusion that on a public interest scale from one to ten, the headline *Black Customers' Reservation Lost in Restaurant Computer* would probably score a few points below *Fly Swimming in Gourmet Soup*.

"Please hold on, I will call somebody for you," she soothed, pausing between words and playing for time as if I were a lunatic wielding a gun in her face. I almost felt sorry for her.

I heard urgent whispers in the background, and then an angry rumble cutting in, probably one of Tumi's relatives tiring of the same old spectacle. Finally a different voice talked at me, older this time, establishing superiority with her groomed English.

"Hello, this is Charlotte speaking. My colleague has just informed me of the unfortunate misunderstanding. Please accept my apologies and let me assure you that we are going to do our best to rectify the situation."

When I asked why it took a call from a white person to rectify the so-called misunderstanding, she fake-apologised once more and then quickly went on to tell me they had a last-minute cancellation and were now in the lucky position to offer my friends a table in a private dining room. In other words, out of sight.

"I am sure they will be very happy," she said breathily.

Before I could go off at her again, Tumi grabbed the phone back (*it's fine, I'll take it from here*) and disconnected the call.

I looked at the phone in my hand, and then I looked out the window, where the sky had turned all shades of pink and purple with swirls of pale blue, and then your excited voices tumbled all over me, "What's wrong, Mama, why are you shouting? Who were you talking to? Was that Tumi?"

I didn't even consider a cover story. Kneeling on the damp bath mat once again, I explained to you that the restaurant people didn't want to let Tumi and her family eat there at first and that had made me so angry that I shouted at them.

"Is it because they are brown? Is the restaurant racist?" Kal asked, quick and to the point as always.

"I think so, yes; the owner probably told the people who are working there that they must not let black people in," I said, holding out two towels as you climbed out of the bath.

"Well done for shouting at them, Mama." Without giving it another thought you started fighting over who got the red towel, because apparently Lele had sat with her naked bum on the blue one. Lele denied it with spitting indignation.

I quickly offered my germ-free towel, a nagging at the back of my mind. I felt I should have offered you something positive to take out of this story. But there was no upside to what happened here and you already had an all-too-clear understanding of how racism operates.

I often worried I had exposed you too early to a vocabulary no child should have to master; that I had robbed you of the innocence of your childhood back in the days when your eyes still grew big and round with questions too complicated for a simple answer, "Why are white people treating brown people so badly?"

I told you then that I didn't have all the answers but that a lot of white people think they are better, cleverer, and more beautiful than black people, because that's what they were told when they grew up. That they often choose to believe what they have been told because it is easier than asking questions. So they believe lies. One of the lies is that black people are all poor and dirty because they are not as clever as white people. The truth is that many black people are poor because white people have made laws that allow them to treat them unfairly and steal from them.

"What did they steal?" you wanted to know.

"Their land and their homes."

"But how, Mama, how did they do it?"

"Imagine somebody would ring our doorbell tomorrow and then as soon as we invite them in, they would move in and make us live in the garage or on the street. If we complained, they would put us in prison and threaten to kill us. We were only allowed back into our house to clean it for them. But they would only ever give us a little bit of money for our work, so we would stay poor and could never afford to leave."

"Why did the black people not chase them away?"

"I think they tried, but it was too late and the white people came with guns. You need to ask Papa about this, he is better with history."

I remembered this conversation as you leaned against me, smelling like lavender and soap bubbles.

"Mama, are you a racist?" Kal asked, eyes squinting into the twinkle of the fake crystal chandelier, a theatre prop I had found years ago in an antique shop in town, envisioning luxuriously scented night baths in its soft glow rather than kneeling half-soaked on a fluffy rug discussing racism with a seven- and a five-year-old.

Of course I am not, I wanted to protest; how can I be racist, when I love you more than anything in this world? Instead I said, "I am not a racist like somebody who calls you bad names and won't let you into their restaurant. But I grew up with many racist thoughts and ideas other white people in Germany told me were true. That has made me a racist, even though I didn't want to be that person."

You both looked at me at that.

"What thoughts? Did you think you were more beautiful than black people?"

"Not really, I never thought I was beautiful. I never met black people when I grew up in Germany. We didn't even see black people on TV or in magazines. My grandma told me that all black children were poor and lived in Africa. That they didn't have enough to eat and couldn't go to schools. I also learned that princesses are always blonde and never even thought that black children could also be princesses or heroes."

"But can they, Mama?"

"Of course. There always have been lots of kings and queens in Africa. And many heroes, some who were fighting white people during Apartheid. And think of all the black people you know who are strong and clever and beautiful just like you."

"Shaka Zulu!" Kal called out excitedly and then added "Mandela and Tutu" in the same breath.

"Tumi and Kate." Lele wanted to be heard too, and my heart did a little skip at the mention of my friends. "Michael Jackson," she quickly added before Kal could have another say.

"He was beautiful when he was a boy but then he didn't want to be black anymore and changed his body," Kal lectured.

"I know THAT," Lele said, and turned to me. "Mama, how did he change his body? Can I also become white?"

"Why do you want to be white?" I asked with a measured smile, trying to keep the alarm out of my voice.

"Because I want your hair, I don't like my hair."

"But my hair is so limp and your hair is strong and you can do so many things with it that I can't." As I said this, I knew of course that this was not the reality you see, and that my words would not make a dent in the relentless media-machine promoting blond, blue-eyed beauty over everything else. I was afraid you could hear this in my voice.

"I don't like it," Lele insisted, a tired sulk creeping into her voice.

"Well, I love it," I said, cheery like Barney, and at least that much was true.

"Do you know why your hair grows up and white people's hair doesn't?" I asked you.

"No, why?"

"Because in the olden times, when white people lived in caves in Europe where it was colder than Africa, they didn't have clothes and only their hair to keep them warm, so their hair had to grow down their bodies. But African people are children of the sun and their hair grew strong and proud towards the sun so it could give them shade."

"Can I not wear a hat in school then?" Kal giggled.

"Sure," I said as I helped you into pajamas, one pink, one black with green stripes, "but you need to grow your hair a bit longer first."

In the end we left the bedtime story and googled pictures of glamorous black hairstyles, mohawks with razor-sharp patterns on the sides and YouTube tutorials on locks and afros. Lele was fascinated by the self-confident American drawls in the clips, and for a few minutes our world was as it should be.

But I knew that the next day you would see magazines in the shops and books on the shelves and you would watch another movie where no one looks like you. The message of your "otherness" would be drummed into you again and again.

At least for that night, as your giggles planted moist kisses on the skin of my neck and your bodies felt warm and solid in my arms, we were safe.

Tumi told me the next day how she had refused to settle for the "private" dining room and made the manager seat them at one of the free tables in the main restaurant; how they were told to keep their voices down like a bunch of six-year-olds misbehaving in church; how she tried to educate their waitress who cringed and clearly wished herself anywhere but serving that black table; how people openly stared at them throughout the evening and how embarrassed she felt in front of her family members from out of town, who were forced to sit through this experience and pay for it at the end. She told me that her father even left a tip so they wouldn't be further stereotyped as typical black customers.

That morning I sat down in front of my computer for the first time in a long time, and started writing for our dialogue blog. I wrote about how I used my white supremacy (we called it privilege back then, but have since realised that this is too benign a word for the violence that comes with it) to call people out. How what we achieved at the end of the day was not a victory. How we needed to do more as white people in our group. I left it there for us to discuss at our next meeting and then we went on our New Year's Eve holiday, only to come back a few days later to a media storm.

Somehow my blog had made it onto Twitter and Facebook and gone viral.

Our Facebook group had over two thousand new member requests and we had to call an emergency meeting to manage press interest and decide who was going to attend various radio and newspaper interviews.

We also had to set up a schedule to monitor our

ever-expanding Facebook group and deal with trolls and racists before they could cause more harm.

New black people showed interest in our group meetings and we redefined our mission statement to include what we had learned since we first started out so naively and enthusiastically.

Suddenly racist incidents all over Cape Town came onto the public radar. We were called for comments, asked for interviews, and invited onto panels. Our popularity and redirected focus electro-shocked our fragmented group back into life and challenged us to be more real.

32

Shopping While Black

Since I had Nhloso, I have had lots of sleepless nights worrying about all of you and what you will have to deal with while growing up. People see your mother and me together and they can't deal with the idea of us being anything else than servant and madam or white lady and needy black woman. We have gone through so many painful experiences because people do not know how to make sense of our friendship.

One morning after dropping you guys off at school, we went shopping at a nearby Woolworths. Nhloso must have been about three months old.

I was walking just behind your mother attending to him while she was throwing stuff in the trolley. Some guy went to her and asked her if I was with her. I was standing literally three feet away from her and could hear every word that was said. Your mum, in confusion, said, "Yes, we are together," and, "Why do you ask?". He said he was just wondering and quickly walked away. We looked at each other and tried to work out what just happened; something felt wrong. I got more and more upset realising he probably thought I was bothering her, asking her for money. I told your mum and she asked what I wanted to do about it.

We called the manager, describing the incident to her and asking her who the guy was and why he had targeted us. She insisted that nobody fitting that description worked in the shop. I knew straight away she was lying; her story did not make sense.

Something was not right, but I was being made to feel like I was crazy. This had happened to me so many times before, but I had learned to trust my instincts. So I went to the back of the store and eventually found the guy there. He tried to avoid me and disappear behind a staff door, but I threatened to stay outside that door until he'd talk to me. He shifted from one leg to the other, looking left and right for help.

When I asked him what had happened, he kept saying "nothing" and he "was just checking". When I repeated my question in isiXhosa, promising that he would not get into trouble, he finally admitted that his boss had asked him to check whether the "white lady" was OK and that I was not harassing her.

The manager came rushing over, asking what the problem was. I told her this was the guy we asked about and that this kind of harassment was unacceptable. I was fuming with anger because my mere presence was criminalised. Out of options, and obviously trying to avoid a big scene in front of the deli counter, where more and more school-mums where collecting their morning lattes, she apologised and promised she "would talk to him and make sure it won't happen again". There was so much more to be said – how talking to him was not going to solve anything, as it was clearly company policy to protect white women from black harassment; how targeting him was not at all what I wanted – but I had run out of steam.

We left the store, and I climbed into the back of your mother's car, holding Nhloso. I felt like weeping. I felt raw. Your mother did not know what to do or say either. She kept checking on me through her rear-view mirror, looking horrified. We had been there before, faced with ignorant or overt racism, and were used to ranting and raving in anger, or venting in the group, or on our dialogue Facebook platform, maybe quoting something Biko said or even finding some dark humour in these kinds of situations, but this time was different. I was in pain; she was in pain. We didn't have any words to even come close to this pain. All we were able to do was sit in stunned silence and hold the space and the moment. What made this experience so much worse for me was the fact that I had my child with me. My heart broke realising that at three months old, he had already been through his first racist experience. The memory haunts me to this day. I sometimes look at white people who find him cute and play with him and I wonder at what age they will stop seeing him as an adorable baby and profile him as a criminal.

I have known racism all my life and learned to deal with it, sometimes well, sometimes not so well. But now I think about the three of you and I think about Nhloso, and I just want to break down and cry.

33

Facing My Inner Racist

May 2018

There is so much I still want to tell you, so many more stories and memories of us I want to capture for you. Tomorrow will be another chapter, and too soon you will have your own stories to write or tell somebody.

As I am writing this, you are at school. Looking out my office window, I can see rainy skies, a rare event we have come to treasure in our drought stricken city. Today I need to decide what will be the last story I tell you in this book. Is there something important I have left out? Should I end on an uplifting note, with a light-hearted memory?

When I started writing to you a few years ago, I had hoped to find answers for you, for myself, for us in the process. Today I realise I don't have any answers. I don't even know the questions anymore. My not knowing has become the one thing I am certain of, something which scares me and gives me hope at the same time. It means shattering all my certainties of old and opening myself to something new.

For the longest time I tried to keep you safe by holding you close to my whiteness while at the same time exposing you to another world; a world where people your colour get dismissed, ignored, belittled, killed, and otherwise silenced by people my colour.

I feared for you with a burning dread, like a child lying awake in the dark knowing that if I closed my eyes, monsters would come out of the shadows. I tried to stay awake, but in the process I became overtired, melodramatic, saw things that were not there, missed signs I should have noticed.

In my white circles there was growing consensus that I was overdoing things, that I was too hard on myself, too pessimistic, that I should worry less, that I was doing "a good thing" by raising you. Meanwhile, a black mother looked at her baby son, measuring out in pinpricks of fear the time she had left until he would stop being cute to white people and turn into a threat that would have to be dealt with.

I was that mother and I was not. I felt neither here nor there. I felt torn at the seams of my whiteness and your blackness.

Then something happened which confronted me with my worst fears (and this is to be my story to end this story):

Your dad and I went for a walk.

It was the middle of the day and a spur of the moment thing. He was giving me a lift home from work and as we were sitting in slow-moving traffic heading up the hill towards our street, we started reminiscing about the times before "the kids", how we used to set off on early morning or sunset walks crisscrossing the slopes of Signal Hill and Lion's Head, dreaming up our future, unpicking the threads of our past, and sometimes arguing like over-excited four-year-olds, shouting "unfair" at the tops of our lungs and calling each other names, emotions running wild and free in all the untamed space around us, until, out of breath and red in the face, we jostled and giggled all the way back home.

Ten years and three kids later, with the mountain and a few hours of free time ahead of us, going for a walk that day seemed like a good idea. We set off as soon as we got home with a bottle of water in one of your schoolbags – no more adult backpacks in the house – and an enthusiastic Berta barking and leaping and running circles around us.

It was one of those Cape Town winter days that feel like summer to my German sense of seasons: electric-blue sky and no wind, the air clear and fresh like stepping behind a waterfall, and the browns and greens of the mountain sprinkled with bright yellow daisies and the occasional glint of pink or purple blossoms. We walked single file without talking much, slowly making our way along the changed anatomy of familiar paths, past a new patch of green-dotted stubble where there was a fire not so long ago, alongside trees that had gotten taller since our last walk, pointing out the occasional flower to each other, a colourful butterfly, or a landmark of our shared history (*Remember, we used to sit here and watch the sunset when Wilma was a puppy?*).

Alan was a few metres ahead of me, your school bag swinging from his shoulder. We decided to make our way up through a patch of leafy trees along a mountain bike trail that had lots of shade and was halfway between a direct uphill scramble and a tarred road for forestry vehicles. A few minutes into the trail, we came to the familiar steep hump, a bit like a ski-slope, and Alan turned around holding out Berta's lead for me to grab onto so he could pull me up the last few metres.

A bird screeched overhead, a piercing sound like metal grinding on metal, reminding me of long ago train rides. I lifted my head to watch it land, a small barrel dropping out of the sky, into the branches of a silver-leafed gum tree. Gum trees, according to your dad, are alien invaders, similar to colonialists, stealing land and water and killing off indigenous vegetation. I never shared his dislike (maybe it's because I am an alien myself) and secretly enjoyed their firework of scarlet- and yellow-dotted blossoms each summer.

In passing I picked one of the spiky, rubbery leaves and crumbled it between my fingers until it released its strong aroma of eucalyptus oil. The smell and the heat coming off the mountain instantly brought back pictures of snow-covered fields framed by the steamed up windows of a Finnish sauna – and I wanted to throw off my clothes and roll around in the cold.

Alan reached the contour path on the top and called Berta. There was an urgent pitch to his voice and I looked up, scanning the path to both sides of him for mountain bikers, worried Berta might be about to harass somebody. But the path was empty, and I assumed he was simply being cautious. He clipped the lead onto Berta's collar, and motioned for me to hurry. His eyes were focused on something behind me, just over my right shoulder. I felt goosebumps rising on the skin of my neck and sped up the last few metres to the top, reaching for his hand. Then I turned around.

A lone figure covered in clothes that seemed far too bulky for this warm day followed soundlessly maybe ten steps behind me, vaguely menacing, like a soldier in full combat gear hiking through a holiday resort. There was an unease in my stomach I couldn't quite comprehend. In my mind we would just have to hold Berta until the strange wanderer walked past. Then a second man emerged from between the trees. They were both walking towards us now in a steady pace, not even slowing down when Alan called out to them, "Watch out for the dog".

Instead they started running and yelling at us, their voices hot and angry. I couldn't make out the words, and was making up explanations in my head (*they are upset about the dog, they are mistaking us for somebody else*), as if by thinking harmless thoughts, I could influence the course of events. As the scene in front of me slowed into frame-by-frame segments, my eyes dropped to the hand of the nearest man reaching into his pocket, a flash sparking off the blade of a knife. I looked up into his face, my mind still asking questions, while my body turned hot and then cold with understanding.

I couldn't tear my eyes away from his face, as if staying connected to his humanness was the one thing that could save us. They might still walk past us, and Alan and I would carry on our carefree amble past flowers and plump little birds in silver trees. My focus narrowed, blackening the edges of my vision, and all I could see were the dark cracks of his eyes, focused on me with empty precision like a hunter taking aim for a kill. A burn like stinging nettles exploded all over my skin.

"Run!"

Alan's voice jolted me into action and I turned and crashed after him down the mountain, rocks slipping under my feet, blood rushing in my ears, heart hammering. At the same time I was watching myself from a distance, thinking, *This is not right, this can't be happening, surely somebody will stop this ...*

The men (how many more were there?) ran after us and kept on shouting, their voices coming from everywhere. They were closing in on us. Rocks flew past my head. A sob rose in my lungs, but nothing came out. Something crashed into the back of my knees and I fell.

As my legs were pulled from under me in slow motion, and my body, still hurtling downwards, connected with stones and branches, I knew with an almost detached clarity that if I broke something – if I hurt myself badly enough and couldn't get back up immediately – I would not survive. Alan would turn around to help me and they would get to him too. You would come home to an empty house and nobody there to explain.

A hand clamped around my wrist, and Alan was dragging me behind him, sliding and scrambling, until I was back on my feet, running once more.

I heard him shout, "I have no wallet, only water."

The school bag was gone from his shoulder, but they were still coming for us.

Then we were back on the path, first houses in sight, and it was all over. The shouting and stones stopped. We didn't dare slow down until we reached the gate in the fence separating our street from the mountain. We didn't speak. Alan fumbled with the numbers on the lock and a new spasm of fear jolted through me, but then the lock gave and we burst onto the road.

Something snapped inside me and a single sob like a scream escaped. Your dad tried to hug me but I couldn't stop moving, my arms limp by my side, my feet on automatic pilot. Back in the house, he threw his arms around me, "Baby, are you OK?" I cried helpless tears and nodded into his chest.

After a while he let go of me and got his phone from upstairs. I heard him, pumped up with fear and anger, as he called people. Then he went back out to look for our attackers. I lay on my bed, still crying, and sent a text to Tumi and one to Kate. Almost immediately they both phoned me and I recounted first to the one, then to the other, what had happened. My story came out in an avalanche of words and sobs, chunks of terror dislodged from my body turned into words and memories that could be heard and understood.

When you came home later, tumbling in with shrieks and tales and what's for supper, I had calmed down enough, but my body hurt in too many places. You, ever observant, asked me what was wrong and I told you without thinking that I fell at college and hit a metal cupboard. You wanted to see my wounds, and exclaimed over the red and purple scratches zigzagging down my side and the size of my ankle.

"But, Mama," you said, anxiety and mild reproach clouding your eyes and knitting your brows, "you always tell us to be careful. You must look where you walk."

Lele of course wanted to know what the cupboard looked like exactly and where it was standing. Luckily my stumbling answers were drowned out by Nene who jumped up and down excitedly asking if she could touch my blood. Meanwhile Kal looked at me with adult concern and offered hugs and a massage. I laughed so I wouldn't cry. I was home and I was with you. Nothing else would ever matter anymore.

Later, when you were asleep, your dad and I held onto each other, talking in stuttering whispers. We went over every step of the walk, over and over again. What we did, what we could have done, what we should have done, what we didn't do, how we perhaps brought this onto ourselves. We carried on for hours obsessing over every little detail. All I wanted was to be able to stop and be normal again, to go to sleep and wake up with no memory of this day.

"I feel so bad for not protecting you," Alan whispered.

"But you did. You did exactly the right thing, you told me to run, and you got us both out of there," I stumbled over my words.

"I should have let Berta go."

"They would have killed her."

"I should have brought a baseball bat."

"You got us out of there."

Long after midnight, more weary than sleepy, we stopped talking. I took half a bottle of Rescue Remedy and some over-the-counter sleeping pills and lay staring into the dark. When I eventually fell asleep, I found myself back on the mountain, running, slipping, falling, stones crashing around me, zombie-like creatures coming for me in an endless repetitive loop until the wake-up alarm on my phone rescued me.

I felt weak and exhausted. The light was all wrong. Everything around me seemed out of focus and glaring like an overexposed photograph.

After the morning routine (*brush your teeth, what do you want for breakfast, don't forget your jackets*) I went to work, because what else was there to do. I remembered your school project and stopped somewhere on Woodstock Main Road to pop into a fabric shop and get some scraps.

As soon as I got out of the car I became aware of too many people, too close to me. I felt vulnerable and exposed, my instincts telling me to run. I tried to reason with myself, recalling my knowledge of post-traumatic stress, and how none of my fears were based on any real danger. But I couldn't stop my heart from racing and my skin from burning.

When a tall black man walked towards me, I escaped into the entrance of a nearby shop, where I bent over a table with bundles of fabric, breathing in gulps of dusty air.

"Lady," I detected a warning in the woman's voice and looked up, new fear rising in my body.

"Can I help you lady?" she repeated, smiling at me from the elevated counter at the back of the shop. Her long black hair gleamed in one of the spotlights dotted around the ceiling. I told her what I was looking for and she pointed me to a wooden box with scraps of fabric. I randomly picked out pieces of fabric, paid and left.

When I got to the office, I pretended all was normal. A friend called from Germany but I didn't tell her. Your Oma called, and we talked about the weather and you. I couldn't tell her either. I was too afraid of what they would say, that what had happened to me would spark their barely contained fear of the black man. I was worried that I might silently agree.

Today I understand that this fear did not start when I was attacked on the mountain, but was planted in my blood a long time ago in ever-increasing poisonous fragments: the neighbour who scared me off when I was playing with the outside tap in the courtyard of our block of flats (*if you go near that tap one more time, the big black bogeyman will come out and eat you*); St Nikolaus arriving in our festive lounge before Christmas with Slave Ruprecht in chains, his face black as coal, grunting and threatening to stuff us bad children into the sack he had slung over his shoulder, my little brother shaking and sobbing next to me, his damp hand clinging to mine, as St Nikolaus interrogated us (*have you been bad little children?*); the game we played aged seven (*Who is Afraid of the Black Man*) when we ran across the schoolyard, always the "black man" chasing us; a fairy tale where a child got dipped in black ink so the world would forever see her sins; my grandmother looking at my wedding picture, exclaiming, "Thank goodness he is white!"

My deeply ingrained terror of the black man had finally caught up with me. Before the attack I had come to understand my unconscious racism in an abstract way. After what had happened on the mountain, it burned under my skin and simmered in my blood. I had managed to save my life from my attackers, but I could not outrun my inner racist. In the days and weeks after the attack, I felt for the first time that I had made a mistake by adopting you and that I was not fit to be your mother.

I cannot say that I have made peace with my inner racist, but I have come to acknowledge and accept her existence in the same way I would perhaps come to live with a disability. I try to be realistic about my limitations. I try not to beat myself up for something I had no control over. I make mistakes and I learn every day. Tomorrow I will do better.

There never was (or ever will be) a point in my life when I could walk away from my whiteness onto a path leading to absolution. I know today that there will always be moments when I cannot even switch perspectives, because what I see and do will forever be framed by my whiteness. How we experience this world will always be separate from each other. I have no certainty, no final wisdom, no truth for you to take from this story.

What remains is my flawed and endless love for you.

You didn't come to me through my body, but you are a part of me, just as I will always be a part of you. My hope is that this story, and others I will tell you, will one day give you a sense of comfort, warmth and belonging, a quilt lovingly stitched together from scraps of fabrics, each holding a special meaning or a memory.

Acknowledgements

I always read the acknowledgements at the end of a book, and I imagine the author sitting with their final manuscript, reminiscing over the process and the many people who brought them to this point. I cannot believe today is my turn.

I'll start at the beginning, when this book began as a creative exercise, and then turned into something bigger. The person who first coached me through my writing, gave me much needed deadlines and then pushed me to go further, Mike Nicol (and lovely Claire, for your co-reading and helpful first edits), thank you!

To my friends far and close who read excerpts, encouraged me and are a part of my story: my "Schatzilein" Anke, Ingmar (of the chocolate stain), Jurgen (you know you are my family, sorry for only featuring you as "the boy who cheated"): so much love!

My dialogue friends past and present: I salute each and every one of you. Thank you for being such an important part of my life, for sitting through the discomfort of reading my one-sided summaries of our first four years together and for allowing me to go ahead.

Tumi and Vicky, you're in a league of your own, there is not enough space here!

Thank you to Colleen Higgs from Modjaji for taking a chance on me and for trusting me to trust my instincts. To my editor, Emily Buchanan, ohmygoodness!! The dedication, heart and skill it takes to immerse oneself in another's story, to breathe and live and relive that story for weeks on end. Your ability to deliver criticism without frills or fear ("unnecessary, melodramatic, we get it") made me wince and LOL at the same time. Thank you for being the person who looked at my book-baby with a loving but realistic eye.

Lastly to Alan, my rock, my best friend and best papa in the world. For listening to every chapter before I sent it off, for the tears and the laughs and for believing in me more than I believe in myself.

Martina and Tumi (photograph Marike Herselman)

Tumi Jonas-Mpofu

Born and bred in Gugulethu, South Africa, Tumi grew up in the last years of Apartheid, grappling from an early age with issues of social injustice and racism. Motivated to understand and challenge herself and those around her, she co-founded "This Dialogue Thing", studied psychology and took up boxing. She recently submitted her master's thesis and lives with her partner and their child in Somerset West.

Printed in the United States
By Bookmasters